Strength-based Lean Six Sigma

This book is dedicated to my parents, Zipi and Avner (may he rest in peace), who have always supported me in discovering my strengths and in pursuing my dreams. Thank you for everything that you have done (and continue to do...on the ground and from above)

Strength-based Lean Six Sigma

Building positive and engaging business improvement

David Shaked

KoganPage

LONDON PHILADELPHIA NEW DELHI

Publisher's note

Every possible effort has been made to ensure that the information contained in this book is accurate at the time of going to press, and the publishers and authors cannot accept responsibility for any errors or omissions, however caused. No responsibility for loss or damage occasioned to any person acting, or refraining from action, as a result of the material in this publication can be accepted by the editor, the publisher or any of the authors.

First published in Great Britain and the United States in 2014 by Kogan Page Limited

2nd Floor, 45 Gee Street	1518 Walnut Street, Suite 1100	4737/23 Ansari Road
London EC1V 3RS	Philadelphia PA 19102	Daryaganj
United Kingdom	USA	New Delhi 110002
		India

www.koganpage.com

© David Shaked, 2014

The right of David Shaked to be identified as the author of this work has been asserted by him in accordance with the Copyright, Designs and Patents Act 1988.

ISBN   978 0 7494 6950 4
E-ISBN   978 0 7494 6951 1

British Library Cataloguing-in-Publication Data

A CIP record for this book is available from the British Library.

Library of Congress Cataloging-in-Publication Data

Shaked, David.
   Strength-based lean six sigma : building positive and engaging business improvement / David Shaked.
      p. cm.
   ISBN 978-0-7494-6950-4 (pbk.) – ISBN 978-0-7494-6951-1 () 1. Organizational change. 2. Total quality management. 3. Organizational effectiveness. I. Title.
   HD58.8.S474 2013
   658.4'013–dc23
                                                                                              2013026095

Typeset by AMNET
Printed and bound in India by Replika Press Pvt Ltd

CONTENTS

ACKNOWLEDGEMENTS

The topic of Strength-based Lean Six Sigma and this book would not be here without the support, encouragement and help of several teachers, other professionals, colleagues and friends. Throughout my journey of discovering, experimenting and developing this topic, several people shared their thoughts, wisdom and suggestions as well as encouragement to carry on. I would like to acknowledge the help of some of these people:

My Lean Six Sigma learning journey began at Johnson & Johnson where I completed the Master Black Belt certification programme and worked on several key business-improvement projects. There were several leaders and trainers who supported and encouraged me along the way, as well as teaching me many important lessons. I would like to acknowledge some of my former colleagues there: Alan Dowie, Thom Fish and Scott Lovin who introduced me to the area of (classic) Lean Six Sigma, sponsored my development and taught me most of what I know as a Master Black Belt.

Moving a few years forward to the time I was introduced to Appreciative Inquiry, I would like to thank Jane Magruder Watkins and Mette Jacobsgaard who introduced me to this topic in their excellent Appreciative Inquiry Foundations workshop. I will always remember how at the end of their workshop, I asked Jane whether she knew anyone else who was combining Lean Six Sigma with Appreciative Inquiry. Her response was simple yet powerful: 'No David, I don't – I'd like you to start it!' That encouragement and her ongoing support helped start the journey. My understanding of Appreciative Inquiry was further enriched by excellent thought leaders and experienced practitioners I have had the pleasure to learn from and work with including: Barbara Sloan, Tony Silbert, Maureen (Mo) McKenna and Liz Workman.

Other important contributors to my learning journey of strength-based approaches to change were Mark McKergow and Jenny Clarke who introduced me to Solution Focus. Their deep knowledge, coaching and support were invaluable, and Mark also contributed his insights to this book.

Through the Strength-based Lean Six Sigma LinkedIn group that I started, I was able to connect with other 'thinking and travel partners'. Several people shared their questions, ideas and thoughts with me and with the group. I would like to thank them all for their active engagement. It would be impossible to name everyone, but the following members were my key thinking partners: David Hansen, Nicolas Stampf, Jeremy Scrivens, Joe Dager, Colin Jones, Nick Dayton and Kicab Castenda-Mendez. Their ideas and questions helped shape parts of the book and make it better. In addition, David, Nicolas and Jeremy contributed their case stories and tools to the book.

Excellent career coaching from Ros Toynbee helped me discover my passion for writing. Further strength-based coaching from Gill How (who also introduced me to my first Strength-based Lean Six Sigma client) helped shape my thinking and approach to writing the book. The writing task itself was supported by my diligent and supportive editor and proofreader, Shelagh Aitken, who provided countless useful suggestions and ensured I dotted all the i's and crossed all the t's!

Of course this book would not be here without the support of Kogan Page. I would like to thank my editors Martina O'Sullivan and Liz Barlow who supported me throughout the commissioning, writing and publishing journey.

I know that in this short summary, I have missed others who supported me along the way and I would like to extend my appreciation and gratitude to them as well.

Introduction

Never before has there been such a strong call for a culture of continuous improvement in the private and public sectors across the global economy. In these challenging times the appetite to discover how to do this better has never been greater. Process improvement has been developed over the last 100 years and, as a result, we know more about the challenges of implementing and sustaining a culture of continuous improvement across organizations than ever before. These challenges are particularly apparent when trying to expand continuous improvement initiatives or projects to a complete culture across organizations so that continuous improvement becomes the 'way work is done'. While Lean or Six Sigma projects or short-term interventions can be very successful in the short run, sustaining the improvements gained and instilling the values, ethos and culture of Lean Thinking and Six Sigma is elusive and easy to miss.

The traditional view is that the best method for improving the way processes in our organizations work is to understand in great detail what does not work well at present. The next step is to find a solution to the problem or its root cause and, finally, to implement it.

We were also taught to develop a vision about a desired future state (typically based on 'best practices') for our processes – followed by a focus on bridging the gaps between the 'as is' and the desired 'to be' states. Both approaches create a continuous focus on the gaps, inadequacies and weaknesses of our processes, systems and people. Admittedly, these approaches to organizational change and improvement have served us fairly well over many decades by driving significantly greater efficiency and quality in manufacturing and other processes. However, there are well-documented examples of failures in driving improvement culture. For example, even Toyota, the source of the Toyota Production System (TPS) that laid the foundations to many of the principles and tools in the Lean tool box, has experienced several highly publicized challenges in recent years that exposed weaknesses and inconsistencies in the way its TPS philosophy was implemented. These included a well-publicized slow response to the discovery of defective car parts installed in millions of cars around the world, as well as other glitches in its supply chain and customer service. These experiences exposed difficulties in truly responding to customer demand on time, in contradiction to the well-known principle of 'Just in Time'.

> Just In Time (or JIT): a manufacturing philosophy that strives to reduce in-process and finished goods inventories by responding to customer demand and by producing what is required exactly when it is required. JIT processes rely on clear, visible signals from customers and between different points in the supply chain. The main objective in setting up JIT processes is an improvement in the return on investment by freeing capital that is normally tied to parts and finished goods inventories.

In addition, transferring the TPS culture that worked well in Japan to US manufacturing plants proved tricky. In another example, the spotlight and high profile given to Six Sigma at General Electric (GE), a corporation highly instrumental in promoting it, shifted to other priorities shortly after Jack Welch's retirement and succession by Jeffery Immelt.

Strength-based Lean Six Sigma: a different way

Most applications of Lean Thinking and Six Sigma assume that there is a 'perfect state' for each organizational process, and that the current state deviates from the 'perfect state' due to inefficiencies and waste.

FIGURE 0.1 The impact of deficit-focus improvements vs strength-based change

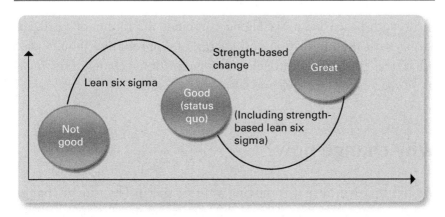

This way of thinking means that, in order to improve our processes, we have to focus on the identification of gaps between the current state and the desired/perfect state (this is called 'deficit focus'). The next step is to find root causes for these gaps and fix them in the hope of making a sustainable improvement. At best, this approach takes you back to a state of status quo ('good') where expectations are met but rarely exceeded.

The strength-based approach to process improvement has a different focus. Instead of focusing on what is broken and inefficient, it helps management and staff identify what is already working efficiently and generates value in existing processes and systems (this is called 'strength focus'.) They then define ways to grow and expand those parts and implement good practices elsewhere. This focus on the search for and growth of existing efficiency enables new ideas to emerge and supports implementation of process improvements by raising confidence and energy levels. The strength-based approach to Lean Six Sigma is more natural to work with and more sustainable in the long term. The deficit focus of traditional Lean tends to weaken the system – even when it is successful – because it instils doubt and despair by giving unbalanced attention to waste and by amplifying inefficiencies.

In every organization there is a wealth of knowledge and practical experience about efficient and value-adding ways to work. This approach has better chances of success as it relies on existing good practices and internal knowledge rather than introducing 'solutions from elsewhere'.

Strength-based Lean Six Sigma combines the rigour of Lean Six Sigma with the innovation and energy of Appreciative Inquiry and other strength-based approaches to organizational change, creating a more successful, inclusive and sustainable result.

Why change now?

We live in a world that is moving at great speed. The rate of change and innovation is faster than ever. There is simply no time to collect data, analyse it, identify root causes and fix them. By the time we have completed this cycle, reality will already have shifted and we are likely to find new problems. In addition, this fast pace also means that we struggle to sustain the improvements we were able to achieve or continuously drive the importance of waste and defect elimination. Motivation and energy – so essential for change – are likely to wane.

The alternative approach of bridging gaps does not offer a solution either. Focusing attention on best practices (introduced from elsewhere), and on current gaps against those best practices, distracts staff attention and does not encourage engagement across the organization or sustainability of existing good practices.

The benefits of the strength-based approach

A strength-based approach to Lean Thinking and Six Sigma creates a committed and focused team working on an improvement initiative with a keen search for possibilities rather than problems. Observing any process with this different 'lens' invites them to start looking for the strengths and opportunities of the process, and to use this information to achieve the desired improvements confidently. Focusing on what works raises energy and motivation. Creativity is higher than that generated by following traditional improvement methods, and innovation is easier to achieve. The ideas for improvements generated through this approach are strong, as well as based on reality and knowledge from within the organization.

Because the process of improvement is no longer accompanied by the negative feelings associated with waste and defects (even if this association is only implicit, it is always present with classic Lean Thinking or Six Sigma), there is a higher degree of participant engagement and sustained energy towards improvement.

Leveraging current or past knowledge as well as accessing experiences and successes from within the system are great resources for the next generation of improvement initiatives. They also provide motivation to everyone towards the challenges and opportunities ahead.

Teaching improvement teams and all members of the organization how to find what is value-generating for customers drives them to consciously or unconsciously seek ways to deliver even more value to customers – isn't that what we're all about?

What is in this book?

This book is your first-hand opportunity to learn more about this application of Lean Six Sigma. It also explores ways to create impact far beyond the minor cost savings achieved through conventional Lean Thinking and Six Sigma projects.

This book starts with a brief overview of the key methodologies underpinning the Strength-based Lean Six Sigma approach. We start with an overview of the common approaches to business and process improvement – Lean Thinking and Six Sigma as well as some of the historical developments that led to the creation of these two popular approaches.

We then move on to reviewing some of the popular strength-based approaches to change, including underlying principles and areas of practice. Although this book focuses on the application of Appreciative Inquiry to Lean Six Sigma, I will cover the other strength-based approaches, and show how they help extend the practice even further.

Next, we will build bridges between the two approaches, beginning with the story of how I made the first few connections. This is followed by the development of robust foundations and the linking of the two paradigms, describing where the two approaches connect. Most practitioners of both approaches can easily identify how they differ but struggle to find the similarities between them. I will build useful bridges between deficit-based and strength-based problem solving.

You may wonder why you should bother practising this approach. I hope the benefits I identify are enough to convince you of the value of combining the approaches. I will also share some of the ways to apply this thinking at different levels of the organization or improvement initiative (the whole organization, a specific process, a team or using a tool for analysis or thinking). I include a few examples of the relevant tools, a few stories from my practice and case studies from other practitioners, and some hopes for the future of Strength-based Lean Six Sigma.

Who is this book for?

If you are a business leader, my hope is that you will find the concepts in this book intriguing enough to explore within your organization. You can apply this thinking to your organization and approach it with a strength focus rather than a deficit focus. This book will give examples using language and tools you may well be familiar with. Using this thinking in your interactions will help you to engage with your business and people in a much more constructive way.

If you are leading an internal improvement team (sometimes this role is called a 'deployment champion' or a 'business improvement leader',) my hope is that by reading this book you will expand your awareness of the possibilities beyond classic Lean Thinking or Six Sigma, and recognize how some of the practices suggested here can get you to your desired destination of quality, efficiency and continuous improvement faster and much more easily with more energy, creativity, engagement and improved sustainability.

I am confident that you will, at the very minimum, try a pilot of this approach.

If you are a trained Lean Six Sigma resource (a Six Sigma belt, a Kaizen/'work out' facilitator, a Lean Sensei or any other term used in your organization for such resources), this book aims to give you a fresh approach to using the tools and processes you are already familiar with. It will also give you different, new tools. Most of all, I hope you gain access to a new way of thinking about the processes and people you are working with in your daily pursuit of improvements. You will find that by using this different 'lens' for processes and people you are able to engage others better and elicit new and useful ideas for improvement.

Finally, if you are an external consultant you will gain two benefits from reading this book:

If you are a strength-based practitioner working with an organization that uses Lean Six Sigma as their primary or key approach to improvement, this book will help you with concrete examples and tools that bridge your way of thinking and operating with the 'mode of operating' inside the organization. You will be able to better understand your clients and support them with their improvement goals.

If you are an external Lean or Six Sigma resource supporting organizations with their change initiative, I hope this book will extend your understanding and use of the tools and methodologies you are already comfortable with and use successfully. As external consultants, the best way to improve the value to clients is by continuously learning and improving our ways of working, bringing them in line with the best practice available in the market and extending ourselves beyond our practice comfort zone.

This book is not intended to be a starting point in learning about the change and improvement methodologies underpinning the practice of Strength-based Lean Six Sigma such as Lean Thinking, Six Sigma, Appreciative Inquiry, Solution Focus or Positive Deviance. While I do provide an overview of these approaches in two separate chapters (Chapter 1 Approaches to Organizational Change and Process Improvement; and Chapter 2 Strength-based Approaches to

Change), this book does not cover the depth of learning and experience required to practise any of these methodologies. There are many excellent books, learning resources and courses available for this. I therefore assume that readers are already familiar or experienced with some of these methodologies (either advanced practitioners of Lean Six Sigma or any of the strength-based approaches to change) and are seeking ways to bring them together or expand their current practice. If that is your goal, this book is for you!

Navigating this book

This book has five parts that follow the common 5D framework of Appreciative Inquiry. The first part, 'Define', explores what is already known at the start of this journey and identifies the emerging topic of Strength-based Lean Six Sigma, the topic I wish to introduce and develop in this book. Next, the 'Discover' part of this book will explore and uncover 'the best of what is' by identifying what works or has worked well in the past, and what the positive core is that will enable us to create the practice of Strength-based Lean Six Sigma. The third part, 'Dream', uncovers 'the best of what can be' by proposing potential connections between the principles of Lean Six Sigma, new Lean Six Sigma processes and possible applications of the strength-based approach to performance metrics. The 'Design' section proposes some of 'what should be'. I will do so by looking at the potential of taking the strength-based thinking and the ideas of the 'Dream' section to a more practical, on-the-ground level and proposing concrete ways forward. Finally, the 'Deliver/Destiny' part will focus on 'what will be'; in it, I provide tips for moving forward as well as case studies from around the world. I also touch on the potential for further developments in this area.

It may be tempting to jump straight into some of the practical tools and proposed ways forward, and you can certainly do just that. However, reading through the different parts and, in particular, reflecting on some of the guiding questions included along the way will help you reconnect with your particular past experiences, build a solid base of knowledge and gain the ability to create your own unique ways of applying this exciting approach.

Enjoy the journey of discovery!

PART ONE
Define

This part will explore what is widely known in Lean Thinking and Six Sigma, and what is widely known in strength-based change. By doing so, we will uncover the potential of a combined approach to process improvement – Strength-based Lean Six Sigma – with roots in both operational efficiency and the approaches to strength-based change.

Chapter 1 provides an overview of the quality and efficiency movements and their current leading methodologies, Lean Thinking and Six Sigma, while Chapter 2 covers the leading approaches to strength-based change, Appreciative Inquiry, Solution Focus and Positive Deviance. Can these two very different worlds of practice and thinking merge to form a powerful combination?

Approaches to organizational change and process improvement

The journey towards improved organizational performance and process productivity has a long history and many notable milestones. In this chapter I will quickly review the key developments along this journey as well as provide an overview of Six Sigma and Lean Thinking, which are specifically relevant to the topic of this book.

Process improvement – historical context

One can say that the journey towards greater efficiency started in the early 1900s with Frederick Taylor, who is widely considered as the originator of management consulting. Taylor's work around scientific management, which defined the role of management and employees, as well as his famous time studies, which were later combined with Frank and Lillian Gilbreth's motion studies, continue to influence the drive towards efficiency to this day. Although modern management and improvement approaches tend to shy away from Taylor's work, some of his discoveries and ideas are still the bases of current practices.

Time and motion studies (or methods engineering): an integrated approach to work systems and procedures improvement that involves the study of the time and movements required to complete a task in a production process in order to improve them and define a standard approach.

The next obvious milestone in this journey can be linked with Henry Ford's efforts to mass-produce cars in the 1920s. Ford introduced the concepts of task specialization, standardization and mass-production. The 1930s brought us the focus on measurements, data analysis (through statistics) and quality control.

Following the end of the Second World War, the next wave of innovation in the area of organizational improvement emerged. In Japan, Toyota started its journey of development of the Toyota Production System (which later formed the basis and core of Lean Thinking). Some of the most prominent tools and approaches we regularly use or refer to in Lean Six Sigma emerged from Toyota. They include problem solving through the 'five whys', continuous improvement (Kaizen), 'Just In Time' production and waste elimination. From 1950 and onwards, William Deming, also in Japan, was busy developing the drive to quality using statistical analysis, root cause analysis, variation reduction and process control.

The late 1970s and early 1980s brought the concepts of TQM (Total Quality Management) and the Japanese Management Systems (with their unique focus on flexibility and quick response to external changes). Many firms around the world, in particular the Western world, attempted (with varying degrees of success) to adopt these operational systems.

The 1980s also brought us an increasing focus on automation and the power of IT. Automation created a new wave of operational change when organizations found more efficient ways of performing many tasks by using information systems and automated processing.

Two more key developments in the 1980s are worth a mention here. First, the science of complexity started getting attention as did the Theory of Constraints (TOC) developed by Goldrat.

Second, the late 1980s brought the introduction by Motorola of its set of quality improvement tools named Six Sigma. It was only when GE adopted Six Sigma as one of its key strategies that the approach started gaining wider attention.

The 1990s continued to build on the trends of the 1980s by introducing Lean Thinking (based on Toyota's Production System and further work on the principles and tools by Womack and Jones). In parallel, we see the Business Process Re-engineering (BPR) movement developing and a growing appetite for outsourcing or offshoring work deemed as 'non-essential' or 'too costly to perform' in the West. Another great development from the 1990s is the introduction of the term 'balanced scorecard', which aims to provide a well-balanced view of the state of an organization. This was done by providing key performance metrics representing the financial, operational, human and environmental aspects of the organization.

The early years of the 21st century saw a huge expansion in the practice of Six Sigma and Lean Thinking across the world. This expansion included for-profit organizations around the world as well as public sector and even some not-for-profit/social organizations. Both Lean Thinking and Six Sigma were no longer limited to applications in manufacturing or supply-chain environments, but rather covered the whole of the organization, impacting HR just as much as IT, finance and sales. The lines of distinction between Lean and Six Sigma have blurred, and many leaders and practitioners now use the combined term Lean Six Sigma, containing the principles and tools of both practices.

Developments in organizational change and change management

While all this great development on the efficiency and effectiveness/quality side was happening, equally impressive developments occurred in the area of organizational change.

At the time of great post-war development in Japan, the completely new area of practice called OD was being thought of and created in the United States. The science of organizational development focuses on helping people, teams and whole organizations cope with, drive and thrive through change in order to keep their organizations and systems alive and competitive. The initial work started in the mid-1940s with Kurt Lewin in the United States and in parallel by the Tavistock Institute (founded in 1946; www.tavinstitute.org) in the UK. New concepts such as 'action research' (coined by Lewin in 1944) and 'group dynamics' surfaced. These were further developed in the 1960s by Tuckman's work (1965) on group processes and psychology. The 1970s and 1980s brought the 'change management' approach with clear models and tools on driving organizational change. In parallel, another management process was being developed – 'project management'. Both these approaches shared many aspects commonly seen in the world of organizational efficiency – the belief that change is linear, mechanistic and can therefore be 'managed' tightly. Both change management and project management tend to start with a given problem, a leader's vision or a 'burning platform', and drive the change journey by solving or overcoming obstacles, gaps and problems.

The late 1980s and onwards brought us the Appreciative Inquiry approach to change, which unlike its predecessors claimed that change is best driven by recognizing the best of what is, developing a shared vision of the 'best that can be' and driving forward 'what should be'. Appreciative Inquiry is based on the action research model developed by Lewin, but has a distinctively different focus (or 'lens'). In Chapter 2 I will cover the topic of Appreciative Inquiry in more detail.

To close this overview of organizational change, the 1990s and 2000s brought a huge development in organizational development (OD) including many different models and tools at multiple levels (the individual level, the group level and the whole organization level). In addition, new dialogue-based methods of intervention and problem solving emerged, and performance coaching became widely known and used. Finally, the science of complexity and the practice of large-scale change saw great advances.

At this stage, you may ask why are the developments in OD relevant in this conversation (beyond the reference to Appreciative Inquiry)? OD primarily focuses on the human and systemic side of change. As we now know and widely accept, operational change requires the engagement, support and wide involvement of the people within organizations and teams working on improvement objectives. It is always useful to consider the human factors when considering operational change.

Six Sigma

Six Sigma seeks to improve the quality of process outputs by identifying and removing the causes of defects and minimizing variability in manufacturing and business processes. This is done by employing a set of quality management tools, including statistical methods. The term 'Six Sigma' comes from a field of statistics known as 'process capability studies'. Originally, it referred to the ability of manufacturing processes to produce a very high proportion of output within defined specification (as derived from customers' requirements). Processes that operate with 'Six Sigma quality' produce long-term defect levels below 3.4 defects per million repetitions. Six Sigma's implicit goal is to improve all processes to that level of quality or better.

Six Sigma originated as a set of practices designed to improve manufacturing processes and eliminate defects, but its application was subsequently extended to other types of business processes as well. In Six Sigma, a defect is defined as any process output that does not meet customer requirements, or (in the case of internal processes) an output that could lead the final outcome of a process to not meet customer expectations.

Six Sigma is based on the following underlying principles:

- Continuous efforts to achieve stable and predictable process results (ie reduce process variation) are of vital importance to business success.
- Operational business processes can be measured, analysed, improved and controlled.
- Achieving sustained quality improvement requires commitment from the entire organization, particularly from top-level management.

What sets Six Sigma apart from previous quality improvement approaches? Six Sigma has a much clearer emphasis on achieving measurable and quantifiable financial returns from any project. It instils a special support infrastructure consisting of 'Champions', 'Master Black Belts', 'Black Belts', and 'Green Belts' (varying levels of expertise) to lead and implement projects, and highlights the role of leadership. Any decisions should be made on the basis of verifiable data, rather than assumptions and guesswork.

Each Six Sigma project carried out within an organization follows a defined sequence of five steps normally referred to as DMAIC. They include:

- Defining the problem, and setting the project goals.
- Measuring current process performance and collecting relevant data about potential root causes.
- Analysing the data to investigate and verify cause-and-effect relationships. Determine what the relationships are, and attempt to ensure that all factors have been considered. The analysis process should yield an identified root cause of the defect under investigation.
- Improving or optimizing the current process by introducing changes that reduce or solve the impact of the identified root cause.
- Controlling/monitoring the newly changed process to ensure that no deviations from expected results occur and that the new process is stable.

Lean Thinking

When we think of our processes as 'lean', we mean that all our resources are used to deliver value to the end customers (as they define it) and nothing else. This value has to 'flow' through the value chain without any interruption. All activities that are not directly support-ing the creation and delivery of value should be considered as waste and therefore reviewed for potential elimination. In other words, Lean is focused on getting the right things to the right place at the right time in the right quantity, while achieving perfect work flow that is dictated by customers' 'pull' of these goods or services. All of this has to be done while minimizing waste, and staying flexible and able to respond to change. Like Six Sigma, Lean originated in and focused on the manufacturing floor and the supply chain. Over the past 10 years or so, Lean has expanded to services and internal support processes in organizations, and we can now see Lean implementation in hospitals, call centres and banks among many other service organizations.

Lean has a set of principles (we will touch upon them later in this book) that emphasize the importance of value, flow and continuous improvement. Different practitioners put a different emphasis on flow versus value.

Some commonly used Lean tools and techniques include: 5S, Kaizen (loosely translated as 'continuously improve' or 'change for better'), SMED (Single Minute Exchange of Dies), Kanban, Seven Wastes, Value-Stream Mapping and Takt Time. There are many other useful tools in the Lean toolbox.

Commonly used tools in the Lean Thinking tool box:

Five S: a process of keeping the workplace ready for use by having a discipline with five workplace practices that begin with S in Japanese (and in their common English translations). They are: Sort; Set in order; Shine; Standardize; and Sustain. The purpose of 5S is to optimize the workplace in a way that makes it easier to perform all tasks in the future. It also enables the important Lean idea of 'visual management' to be done more effectively.

Seven Wastes: Waste is any activity that consumes resources but creates no value for the customer. The seven categories of waste as identified in this tool are: 1) Defects; 2) Overproduction; 3) Unnecessary Transportation; 4) Waiting; 5) Inventory; 6) Unnecessary Motion; and 7) Over-processing. The purpose of using the seven wastes is to identify and eliminate waste in processes, thus providing greater value to customers.

Takt Time: The average rate at which a deliverable item is required in order to meet customer demand. Takt time is used to help create balance in processes and to calculate the resources required to efficiently complete a process.

One value of the Toyota Production System that is particularly important to mention in our context is 'respect for people'. This normally comes down to: respecting all stakeholders; building trust; and placing a special emphasis on teamwork.

Although LEAN is often portrayed as a collection of tools to manage and improve processes, it is firstly and mostly a whole-system management philosophy, and therefore the adoption of Lean in an organization stipulates a significant culture change at all levels. Such a complete culture change is what separates truly successful Lean organizations from other organizations that have tried to run 'lean initiatives' with more local focus (even if these initiatives were proven to be very successful).

Lean Six Sigma

The Lean Six Sigma methodology views Lean Thinking, which focuses on process flow and waste elimination, and Six Sigma, with its focus on process variation and defects, as complementary approaches aimed at driving 'business and operational excellence'. In recent years, there has been a greater tendency to use the combined term (and hence the combined philosophies and tool boxes) rather than specifically choosing one or the other.

Summary

In this chapter we reviewed the historical context of the key developments in the drive towards organizational efficiency from the early works of Taylor and Ford, through to the progress made in the area of organizational development, and finally the emergence of Lean Thinking and Six Sigma. It highlights the parallel journeys of discoveries both on the operational and human sides of the organization. While the operational side has brought us many useful tools and thinking approaches to problem solving, the human side helps us understand what motivates people in organizations as well as how to drive change. The practice of Strength-based Lean Six Sigma combines the two and offers an effective balance of human and operational thinking.

In the next chapter, I will explore in further detail the key strength-based approaches to change that have emerged from the practice of organizational development covered in this chapter.

Strength-based approaches to change

There are several strength-based approaches to individual, team and organizational change. This chapter provides a brief overview of the key approaches that influence and inform the strength-based approach to Lean Six Sigma.

First let's define the term 'strength-based'. Essentially the strength-based 'lens' to change is inviting us to find, in each situation or problem:

- what is right, useful, successful, uniquely good or 'alive' that we can build upon;
- what existing assets and resources we can build upon;
- what cases of 'positive deviance' (examples where the problem does not exist) can be spotted and learned from;
- how we can amplify what already works.

This is often compared to the classic 'deficit' or 'gap' approach, which has been practised for much longer than the strength-based approach. The deficit approach typically asks:

- What is wrong, not functioning well or not operating to expected standards?
- What are the existing gaps between our current performance and an 'ideal' situation?

- What problems need solving?
- What are the development and improvement needs?
- What gaps and deficiencies need to be filled?
- What are the root causes to a problem?

A detailed comparison between deficit-based and strength-based problem solving can be found in Appendix A.

The key approaches to strength-based change that inform the practice of Strength-based Lean Six Sigma include:

1 Appreciative Inquiry;

2 Solution Focus coaching;

3 Positive Deviance.

The following is an overview of these approaches in more detail.

Strength-based approach 1: Appreciative Inquiry

"No problem can be solved from the same level of consciousness that created it. We must learn to see the world anew." Albert Einstein

Appreciative Inquiry (AI) is an organizational development approach that actively seeks:

- what is good in an organization; a team or an individual;
- what is working well in the organization;
- when the organization is performing at its best.

The basic idea is to build organizations and processes around what works, rather than trying to fix what does not. It is the opposite of traditional problem solving. Instead of focusing on fixing what is wrong, Appreciative Inquiry focuses on how to create more of what is already working, as well as creating an attractive vision of the desired future. By doing so, we create confidence in people about their ability to deliver positive results because their chosen path for future improvement is based on their own past successes. Future success becomes more visible as well as meaningful.

Appreciative Inquiry is a unique way of asking questions that enable a team or a whole organization to envisage the future. It releases the immense creativity and resourcefulness that is normally hidden (and very rarely tapped into) in each and every one of us. In so doing, it enhances people's capacity for collaboration and change.

A typical Appreciative Inquiry experience follows a five-stage process focusing on:

1 **Define**. Identify the appreciative topic to focus and grow.

2 **Discover**. The exploration of what works (or has worked) well – the best of 'what is'.

3 **Dream**. The envisioning of what could work well in the future – the best of 'what can be'.

4 **Design**. Planning and prioritizing what will actually work well in the future – finding ways to move towards the shared dream.

5 **Deliver**. The implementation of the proposed design.

This five-stage process can be implemented in several different ways. They range from working with a small group on a project or a specific problem/need and all the way to a large, organization-wide gathering called an Appreciative Inquiry Summit.

Appreciative Inquiry was originally based on the following five principles:

1 **The Constructionist principle**. Reality and the future are founded on our own construction, based on our context and fuelled with conversations.

2 **The Simultaneity principle**. Change starts with the first question/inquiry.

3 **The Anticipatory principle**. People and organizations move in the direction of their visions and dreams.

4 **The Poetic principle**. Organizations are like books, being co-authored at every moment. We have the choice of what we inquire into and freedom to choose what to focus on as we create a path to move forward.

5 The Positive principle. Choosing the positive as the focus of inquiry releases positive energy that is useful to drive and sustain the change we want to see.

These principles were set out by David Cooperrider in 1987.

Further principles were defined and added later, including the important principle of Wholeness, which emphasizes the need to bring the whole system into the conversation and respectfully integrate diverse views about a given situation. In fact the topic of this book is an example of the Wholeness principle in action – integrating two seemingly different views for process change and improvement.

We will touch upon these principles and their impact on Strength-based Lean Six Sigma later.

It is important to remember that although the five-stage process described above is very common, it is not the only way to use Appreciative Inquiry. As you will see later on in this book, some of the tools and processes proposed here apply Appreciative Inquiry thinking and its principles in very creative ways.

Strength-based approach 2: Solution Focus coaching

Solution Focus coaching is another strength-based approach to positive change. It can be used with individuals, groups and organizations.

The Solution Focus (SF) approach to problem solving holds that focusing on problems and understanding their root causes is not the best way forward. Instead, the conversation revolves around what's wanted (not what's wrong), moving towards a better future (not trying to avoid a worse future), what is going well (rather than what has gone wrong), what strengths can be found (not weaknesses) and small steps (rather than huge plans). This approach can be summarized in the phrase: 'Find out what works and do more of it.' It is a way of interacting that leads to useful and positive thinking, helping release ideas and action towards progress.

There are a number of key assumptions that underpin solution-focused work:

1 Change is happening all the time. Our job is to identify and amplify *useful* change.

2 There is no one 'right' way of looking at things: different views may fit the facts equally well.

3 Detailed understanding of the 'problem' is usually of little help in arriving at the solution.

4 No 'problem' happens all the time. The direct route lies in identifying what is going on when the problem does not happen.

5 Clues to the solution are right there in front of you: you just need to recognize them.

6 Small changes in the right direction can be amplified to great effect.

7 It is important to stay solution-focused, not 'solution-forced'.

In addition to these assumptions, the SIMPLE framework of principles is the platform for the Solution Focus methodology, first outlined by Paul Jackson and Mark McKergow in their book *The Solutions Focus* (2007). The six principles of this framework are:

1 **Solutions not problems.** Focus your work on the solutions not on the problem.

2 **In-between.** Interaction is the platform for change. 'The action is in the interaction.'

3 **Make use of what's there.** Find out what strengths, resources, solutions and good intentions are available and work with them.

4 **Possibilities.** Many solutions are possible – they may come from past and present experiences or positive hope and expectations about the future.

5 **Language.** Use positive, clear and uncomplicated language.

6 **Every case is different.** Start afresh from the 'here and now' and find solutions that fit *this case*.

Every facet of the SIMPLE framework is important, but the choice of acronym is deliberate. The emphasis given to simplicity is essential to

Solution Focus work. Often clients who go through a Solution Focus experience are surprised by how simple, yet powerful, this approach is in helping them create a path towards solutions even when the starting point is a very 'complex' problem. Practitioners of Solution Focus need to remember that there should be no need to make something more complicated than it already is.

The Solution Focus tools

There are six basic Solution Focus tools to help apply the SIMPLE principles and achieve the solution we are seeking. These six tools are only the basis of a much wider practice of coaching individuals and groups.

The first of these tools is the 'platform'. The platform is typically a point of departure for the process of searching for what works. Establishing the platform early in the change process is essential to support the changes we are going to make. The platform describes what is wanted and why (who might benefit and how).

Next we define the 'future perfect'. This tool describes in detail a future without the problem that we are trying to resolve. In other words, what would be different when the problem has gone?

Drawing up or identifying a 'scale' can help us measure progress on our path to a solution. We typically point out where we currently are on the scale in relation to the future perfect (a score of 10). We also identify what is the next stage on our way forward as well as what will be different or better when we arrive at that stage.

Accumulating 'counters' along the way from the platform to the future perfect is helpful in moving towards the solution or in improving further on the scale. Counters are any resources, skills, know-how and expertise that can help us move towards the solution.

Another important tool is 'affirmation': recognizing and affirming the contributions and progress people are making in the search for solutions.

Finally, 'small actions' are key to finding solutions. Often these small actions will push you further toward a solution by helping you discover new counters.

FIGURE 2.1 The six basic Solution Focus tools

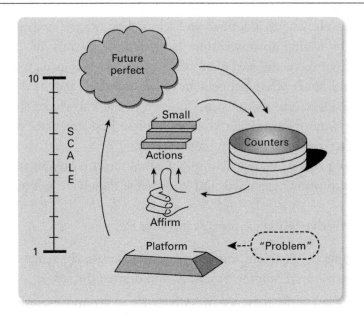

The description of the tools provided above and in Figure 2.1 shows one path or sequence towards a solution using the Solution Focus tools. However, different situations might emphasize different tools. For example, the solution to a strategic problem might be revealed by defining the future perfect. For another problem, finding counters is the key step.

Solution Focus work has spread worldwide and gained a reputation for building useful change, energizing people and enhancing relationships in a very time-efficient way. It is used not only in coaching, but also in OD, team development and day-to-day management.

Strength-based approach 3: Positive Deviance

Positive Deviance advocates that in every community or organization there are a few individuals or groups who have overcome or prevented the problem we wish to solve. The best solution to a pervading problem would come from within the community or organization. In other words, we are utilizing internal 'good practices' from within the system we are working with, rather than introducing 'best practices from elsewhere' identified and selected by external experts. This is done by asking groups within the system to identify the *positive deviants*, observe (in a similar way to the 'go-see' principle from Lean) and study what happens in these situations that is different. They then separate the most useful core of the knowledge acquired and find ways, from within, to expand these best practices, evaluate their effectiveness and disseminate further.

In this process, people within a community or organization are able to tap resources, assets and knowledge they were not aware of before.

The Positive Deviance process has four steps:

1 **Define** the problem, current perceived causes, challenges and constraints, common practices, and desired outcomes.

2 **Determine** the presence of individuals or groups who form a positive deviant to the problem.

3 **Discover** uncommon but successful behaviours and strategies through inquiry and observation.

4 **Design** activities to allow community members to practise the discovered behaviours.

In addition, there is monitoring and evaluation happening throughout the four Ds. The evaluation and monitoring is specifically focused on storytelling, sharing improvements and progress, thus further fuelling the change.

This 4D process is an iterative road map for learning and improvement. Note that although the Positive Deviance process may have similar steps to Appreciative Inquiry, the focus and application are different.

In addition to the 4D process, there are nine principles guiding the Positive Deviance approach to change:

1 The system (either a community or an organization) owns the entire process.

2 All individuals or groups who are part of the problem are also part of the solution and hence the Positive Deviance

process involves all parties who affect the problem. 'Do not do anything about me without me.'

3 The system discovers existing uncommon, successful behaviours and strategies (Positive Deviance inquiry).

4 The system designs ways to practise and amplify successful behaviours and strategies and unleashes innovation from within.

5 Members of the system recognize that 'someone just like me' can get results, even in the worst case scenarios (evidence from within).

6 Positive Deviance emphasizes practice instead of knowledge – the 'how' is more important than the 'what' or 'why'. The Positive Deviance mantra is: 'You are more likely to *act* your way into a new way of thinking than to *think* your way into a new way of acting.'

7 The system creates its own benchmarks and monitors progress.

8 Positive Deviance process facilitation is based on deep respect for the systems we work with, its members, and its culture. Positive Deviance focuses on interactive engagement and capacity to let the community lead.

9 The Positive Deviance process expands existing networks and creates new ones.

As you can see, these principles emphasize self-reliance and asset-based approaches and beliefs.

Shared themes between the key strength approaches

Although the strength-based approaches I describe above come from different sources and, in their early stages, targeted different situations, the practice of these approaches is starting to converge. For example, Appreciative Inquiry started as a quantitative research technique at a whole-system level using unconditional positive questions. These days, many practitioners use Appreciative Inquiry for individual coaching while Solution Focus is regularly used for working with groups and whole organizations. It is also possible to blend the different approaches as they share many common themes. Essentially, they all agree that there is great value in shifting or prioritizing the focus on:

- what is working well/has worked well;
- what helps us/the situation be at its best;
- what we already know;
- what resources are available to move forward;
- what vision we want to move towards;
- where/when does a 'problem' not occur (or occurs to a lesser degree);
- where are the 'positive deviants';
- what we can do right away to move forward.

The shift or prioritization of the above leads to: creativity, resourcefulness, confidence and a clearer way forward!

The differences between the strength-based approaches

While Appreciative Inquiry, Solution Focus and Positive Deviance share many themes, including a particular focus on what is positive in a situation and existing strengths, it is important to also highlight some of the key differences between the approaches:

- Appreciative Inquiry and Positive Deviance place a high level of importance on working with whole systems while Solution Focus advocates that, although working with whole systems is preferable, it is not necessarily the starting point, and that great progress can be achieved in a situation even without the whole system.
- Solution Focus and Positive Deviance start with the present, the 'here and now', while a common starting point in Appreciative Inquiry is gaining knowledge from the past.

- Solution Focus and Positive Deviance highlight the usefulness of positive exceptions or deviants in the present. Appreciative Inquiry practitioners may or may not choose to inquire into the existence of positive deviants in the present.

- Solution Focus emphasizes the importance of staying simple as well as using simple, uncomplicated language. Appreciative Inquiry specifically values more complex and poetic language.

- An important belief in Solution Focus is that small steps and gradual progress usually open a path towards the desired future and are a great way to achieve a greater shift. Appreciative Inquiry does not necessarily focus on smaller steps.

- Positive Deviance emphasizes the value of observation of current good practices as the preferred way to collect useful information. Appreciative Inquiry and Solution Focus prefer the use of inquiry and dialogue as the best ways to tap into internal knowledge of good practices.

Other complementary tools and approaches

There are several other strength-based, positive and dialogue-based approaches to change, as well as tools, that I sometimes incorporate in my practice of Strength-based Lean Six Sigma. Because they are peripheral to the main approaches in my practice, I will not review them here. The following list names just a few:

- **Dialogue-based approaches**: Future Search, World Café, Open Space, OPERA, clean language coaching, 'time to think', Motivational Interviewing.

- **Ways to know ourselves and others at our best**: Positive Psychology, emotional intelligence/EQ, Strength-finder, StrengthScope, VIA, Realise2.

- **Tools**: SOAR (Strength, Opportunities, Aspirations, Results).

As you learn and create your own approach to Strength-based Lean Six Sigma, I encourage you to explore some of the main approaches and complementary tools, and integrate the ones that are most useful to you.

Learning more about strength-based change

To learn more about these strength-based approaches to change, look at the resources section at the end of this book (Appendix B). My best advice to those who wish to expand their knowledge of these methodologies is, where possible, start by having an actual experience of them. This can be done through speaking to an experienced practitioner, participating in a workshop or taking part in an activity that uses these approaches. Once you have had the experience, reading about the approach and the specific tools it uses is easier to grasp.

Summary

In this chapter I have provided an overview of three key approaches to strength-based change in human systems. Each methodology has its unique tools, processes and principles. Some of the principles are shared, while others are unique to the specific approach. If you are not familiar with these approaches, I hope that reading about them has made you curious and interested in learning more. Learning and practising any of these approaches is easy to start with and opens up the potential for a life-long journey of learning and growth.

This chapter also marks the conclusion of the first part of this book. By reviewing the two parallel journeys of development in operational and organizational change, I hope I have raised your curiosity about the potential links between the two worlds of practice in driving organizational improvement. These links, as I will show in the next parts, form the foundations of Strength-based Lean Six Sigma. My hope is that you will find this topic can build bridges between different ways of thinking, and that it will enhance your approach to driving process improvement change initiatives.

Before you move to the next part of the book, I invite you to reflect and choose the topic you are most intrigued by. What would you like to expand your understanding of? The following questions may be useful to reflect on:

1 What in my view is Strength-based Lean Six Sigma?

2 What parts of it am I already familiar with, do I know about, or feel comfortable with?

3 What seems unique, different or fresh about what I have read so far?

4 Which approach to change or improvement am I called to learn more about or experience?

5 Do I want to embark on this learning and change journey?

6 Where should I start? What could be my first step?

7 Which chapter in this book thus far am I most curious about?

PART TWO
Discover

The roots of Strength-based Lean Six Sigma lie in finding the best of what is already known about organizational and process efficiency – integrating the best of Lean Six Sigma practice with the best ideas from strength-based change. This is fully aligned with Appreciative Inquiry's emphasis of continuity in every change effort. Valuing and ensuring the continuity of the best of the past forms the seeds for new developments.

Chapter 3 begins the discovery process with the story of my own journey of discovery and the insights I gained throughout the journey. Chapter 4 explores in detail the potential contribution each of the strength-based approaches to change offers the practice of Lean Six Sigma.

Chapter 5 explores how Lean Six Sigma and Appreciative Inquiry principles can be linked. Finally, this part of the book will finish by helping you explore the positive core of your own knowledge and practice.

The birth of Strength-based Lean Six Sigma

A journey of discovery and emergence

I have worked for several years, as a business improvement and organizational development practitioner, on improving and changing processes and parts of businesses. Years of practising business process re-engineering and Lean Thinking have taught me useful lessons. Many of the improvement projects I worked on relied significantly on people rather than machines, from early work in HR, including improvements to HR processes, through to procurement, sales, marketing, finance and IT: all rely on the people in the organization as their key success factor. I have always kept this fact in mind when approaching efforts to 're-engineer' or 'fix' something.

Strength-based Lean Six Sigma was born as a result of my own journey from focusing on deficit-based problem solving to practising strength-based organizational change. All my experiences to date have been instrumental in the creation of the blended approach that is Strength-based Lean Six Sigma.

Problem-solving experience built, Appreciative Inquiry discovered – now what?

I had built a great track record in the corporate world over several years: I was solving business challenges and concentrating on improving inefficient and wasteful processes. I was using well-tried business improvement approaches such as Six Sigma and Lean Thinking. I also regularly used analytical approaches such as SWOT analysis; gap; stakeholders; and force-field analyses to support change efforts. To monitor the progress made through my own change and business improvement efforts, as well as those of others, I introduced the balanced scorecard, key performance indicators and control charts.

Waste and defects were everywhere I turned! My efforts to eliminate them impacted positively on our customers and on the bottom line. At the same time, and particularly in the role of a Lean Six Sigma Master Black Belt, I was teaching others how to use these approaches so that they could also hunt out waste. There were enough examples of waste and defects to keep us busy forever. In fact, they seemed to pop up like mushrooms!

Then I discovered Appreciative Inquiry!

Being used to identifying the problems in each situation, I was intrigued by the completely different focus of Appreciative Inquiry on how to achieve our dreams by focusing on what was working well and exploring how good we could get. I found myself torn between two seemingly conflicting worlds. While I knew how to methodically solve problems by the classic approaches, I could also see how the positive approach of Appreciative Inquiry released a huge creative resource with the first few groups I tried it on. My big question was how to integrate this fantastic new approach with everything I had been doing before.

At that stage, I felt that my work with Six Sigma and Lean Thinking was 'bad' and that Appreciative Inquiry was 'good', that I had to throw away everything I had learned and experienced until then and restart a new learning journey. All my experience to that date seemed to fundamentally clash in style, language, process and logic with this new way of thinking. For example, how could I connect Appreciative Inquiry's 5D (Define, Discover, Dream, Design and Deliver) process with the DMAIC (Define, Measure, Analyse, Improve and Control) process from Six Sigma, with its specific emphasis on finding root causes for problems through analysis? How could I continue my efforts to eliminate waste while inquiring into what gives life to my organization?

These questions kept confusing me. On the one hand, I loved the energy and creativity Appreciative Inquiry brought by focusing on the strengths and high moments. On the other hand, I did not want to lose the familiar world of process mapping with Post-it notes and deep statistical analysis. I still believed they were useful.

Consulting books and experts from both areas of practice did not seem to help. Great Appreciative Inquiry books highlighted the difference between strength-based and deficit-based approaches without offering ways to bridge the two worlds, while Lean Six Sigma practitioners were quick to point out the *defects* and *waste* inherent in the Appreciative Inquiry process.

Appreciating all my skills and building bridges between them

Over time, I learned more about Appreciative Inquiry. The experience I gained offered a potential solution to my challenge. For example, I learned that the 5D framework, while solid and versatile, is not the only way to apply the approach. Being driven by my desire to be a better practitioner, I gained a deeper understanding and stronger connection to the principles behind 5D. I realized then how important it was to apply these principles to everything I did, both professionally and personally. The conversations I had around the principles of Appreciative Inquiry changed the way I looked at my work and my life. It made them both more meaningful and alive.

I also started appreciating my strengths and best experiences to date, and what I already knew well. This included the strengths and best experiences I had while *practising deficit-based techniques.*

It meant that I started asking myself different questions. Instead of asking how to 'fix' my problem-solving skills in order to create a bridge between my two internal worlds, I started exploring my own strengths.

What did I do well when I worked with Six Sigma and Lean Thinking? What were the most powerful problem-solving experiences I had? What were the best insights I gained when analysing data? What did I like the most? Which tools worked best? What did people I worked with like about these methodologies? What worked well for the organization when I applied them? What was so unique and attractive about these methodologies? What did I wish to see in the future? In other words what 'gave life' to my traditional way of solving problems and where could all of this take me in the future? I started discovering my own positive core!

> Identifying and focusing on the positive core is an important concept in Appreciative Inquiry. The positive core is the collection of the best of our past experiences, key knowledge, underlying beliefs and values as well as great practices that enable our best performance.

The shift of my attention towards what was the 'positive core' in my way of solving problems generated the breakthrough I was yearning for.

All of a sudden, I could see potential bridges and new ways to work with the old methodologies people are so familiar with. To start with, I referred back to the guiding principles behind Six Sigma and Lean Thinking. These principles were actually, to my surprise at the time, very strength-oriented and phrased in positive terms. For example, the reason Six Sigma is focused so much on defect identification and elimination is actually the pursuit of quality; the guiding principle behind Lean Thinking is the desire to deliver the best value to the customer as quickly as possible. All of a sudden there did not seem to be such a dichotomy between the two worlds!

Around this time I was also exposed to, and started learning about, the Solution Focus approach to coaching and change. Solution Focus expanded my strength-based skills even further. It introduced me to a set of tools, assumptions and ways of thinking that was complementary to Appreciative Inquiry, and at the same time was easier to grasp for someone like me who came from the world of deficit problem solving. In fact, one of the biggest breakthroughs I experienced along my journey happened through a 20-minute-long experience of the 'small steps' tool as applied to my own challenge of combining strength-based approaches with Lean Six Sigma. It gave me a unique 'Eureka!' moment full of ideas for the next few steps. One of them was a complete redesign of how I prepared for and facilitated a Kaizen improvement workshop – a new strength-based Kaizen workshop design was born!

The next stage in this journey was to take the tools and techniques from Six Sigma that I liked the most and apply an appreciative approach (or a 'lens') and the principles of Appreciative Inquiry to them. I also had to rethink the questions underpinning these tools. For example: I had enjoyed facilitating groups through process-mapping exercises to gain clarity around a given process. I realized that instead of focusing the group's attention on the waste and problems in the process, I should apply the positive principle by getting them to focus on the parts of the process where value is created and good performance is already achieved. Waste disappears more naturally if people orientate themselves towards ways of increasing the value they generate in any process.

The questions I ask managers, employees and customers as part of the Six Sigma 'Define' stage are focused on trying to find out when the process has worked well in the past, or what they wish to see more of (instead of what they want to reduce or eliminate). Alternatively, I ask them to describe how the situation would look with the problem solved. Another example is the use of the powerful statistical tools and rigour that Six Sigma and the DMAIC model provide to identify root causes of success and ways of amplifying those, instead of studying defects. I also apply the principle of wholeness by involving a wider representation of the system I work with.

Finally, I also realized that I, and the systems I worked with, placed great value on collecting and analysing data. We always sought the lowest points of performance or where inconsistencies occurred – this was where we focused our curiosity and analytical skills, trying

CASE STUDY Appreciative Lean Thinking and problem solving in practice – a case story

My first experience of working with my new strength-based Kaizen approach (and one of the best examples I have to date of the Simultaneity principle in action) was with a rail company. The client asked me, along with my colleague Gill How of Buonacorsi Consulting, to facilitate a process-improvement workshop to reduce the delays to rail services that occurred when faulty carriages were exchanged with serviced ones. The exchange, when not done correctly or in a timely fashion, caused delays to the rail service and a chain-reaction of further delays to other services.

At our first meeting, the head of the department in charge of rail performance provided us with plenty of data points about the delays, their frequency, root causes and their great financial impact on the company. I listened to the story very intently. After all, it felt comfortable to understand in detail all of the data in front of me.

However, for the first time, I felt I was not hearing the complete story. I was curious about something else. It took a while to formulate in my mind what exactly I was looking for. After a while, I asked our client how often the organization changed carriages successfully and on time. A powerful moment of silence followed… The answer our client provided was 'I don't know… I don't think we ever measured it.' A slight, but very prominent breakthrough had just happened!

From that moment on, our conversation took a completely different direction. We were all curious to find out how often the process worked well, what contributed to this success and how we could do more of what already worked.

This single, powerful question was the basis of the workshop we delivered following a new and innovative design, based on Lean Thinking process-improvement workshops I had delivered in the past, but run with an appreciative, strength and value focus. We inquired about best experiences, mapping the process when it worked (guess what… 80 per cent of carriage changes were successfully completed on time). We collected stories and data about the process at its best and asked participants what would make it even better. The questions asked, the evidence sought and the analysis conducted were all different from the normal Lean Thinking approach, and more powerful. The participants' great ideas came from good practices they were already doing or had done in the past.

It was an exciting process to facilitate and observe. It also felt very satisfying personally to reach this point in my own professional development, and to be able to connect my ideas and knowledge in this approach. A new, more appreciative and life-giving way for Lean Thinking process improvement was born!

This positive first success led to more projects and different experiences of combining Lean Six Sigma with strength-based change. Over time, this different way of practising Lean Six Sigma has grown and developed, and has become a new, more generative and complete practice – a practice I would like to share with others.

to make meaning of those situations. From experience, I can now say that changing the focus and directing our curiosity towards 'what works well' can be just as useful, if not more so. In Chapter 9, I apply this thinking to metrics and performance reviews.

These ideas may seem as challenging to other successful problem solvers as they were to me at the beginning. We were trained to assume that in every organization and its various processes there are problems waiting to be identified and solved. What would happen if we approached our improvement efforts with an underlying assumption that every organization and process is a result of an idea that was great in the beginning, and that in every organization or process something works well and delivers value? After all, we can almost always point out areas where our current problems were once a good solution to another problem. The outcome of any given cycle of problem solving lays the foundations of the next problem and is not necessary at all. If we dare suspend our basic suspicion about every organization or process, we may find and access more creative ideas, greater motivation for change, and the innovation that is so essential for survival in the marketplace.

Summary

My experience so far leads me to believe that a strength-based approach to Lean Six Sigma can combine the best of both worlds. It also offers a wider and deeper look for practitioners of both Lean

Six Sigma and of strength-based change. There is no need to look at the two as opposites. This is particularly true when we consider the principles of Lean and Six Sigma and the positive hope they portray. Appreciating the positive core of all the methodologies we have at our disposal and our own positive core as experienced change agents is a useful starting point. Applying new ways of thinking, asking different questions from those we may be used to, looking at a familiar practice we know well with 'fresh eyes' and using strength-based tools can help us expand our understanding of our own practice. We can generate new insights that can guide us in choosing our next steps towards learning and growth.

Appreciative Inquiry can benefit from the variety and rigour of some of the deficit-based models and methodical thinking processes that worked so well for such a long time (provided we use them with different underlying assumptions and direction of inquiry).

At the same time, successful practitioners of the various deficit-based models that have been developed during the 20th century could bring energy and exciting new innovations to these models by applying strength-based thinking to their improvement experiences.

As we move to the next chapter, where I will explore in more detail the contribution each strength-based approach to change makes to the practice of Lean Six Sigma, I invite you to reflect on the following questions:

1 What parts of the journey I described above feel close to the path you have taken in your learning journey?

2 Which insights that I have shared above inspire your curiosity?

3 What stands out for you in my journey?

4 What do you wish to explore further and gain new insights about?

The potential contribution of the strength-based approaches to Lean Six Sigma

ppreciative Inquiry was my starting point in the journey towards Strength-based Lean Six Sigma – a practice that later benefited further from the other strength-based approaches I described earlier, such as Solution Focus and Positive Deviance. In this chapter I will highlight what each of these frameworks can offer process-improvement efforts, and how they complement and add value.

Appreciative Inquiry

In my view, there are three key benefits Appreciative Inquiry can offer to process-improvement initiatives and projects. They are:

1 An emphasis on reframing the topic of inquiry – for example, do we want to learn more about what causes delays to the replacement of faulty carriages or what helps us replace them on time and without problems?

2 Using different sources of information. For example, is narrative as useful as quantitative data?

3 The simultaneity of inquiry and change. Are they separate or are they linked?

The following points explore these questions in depth:

1 Reframing the topic of inquiry

Through Appreciative Inquiry I learned that what we ask determines what we find, and that it is often useful and sometimes crucial to reframe the topic of inquiry before actually starting it. By reframing, I mean focusing on what we want to see *more of*, or *growing* in any particular situation.

Often our business- and process-improvement conversations revolve around what we wish to eliminate or reduce. Although these conversations may be useful, they do not always point us in a useful direction. Asking about what is wanted instead and/or what would make the situation better leads to a more generative way of working with Lean Six Sigma process improvement, and can generate some interesting and creative ways forward. Reframing the topic of inquiry helps us move from 'good' to 'great'. For example, in her book, *The Power of Appreciative Inquiry*, Diana Whitney shares a story about working with British Airways on reducing the number of lost bags for passengers flying across the Atlantic. Her work with the client helped transform the topic of inquiry from 'lost luggage' to 'excellent arrival experience', a more generative topic. The case story on the next page provides another example for the value of reframing a topic of inquiry.

2 Opening the door to different sources of information

Both Six Sigma and Lean Thinking value quantitative data. The frequencies of defects, the cycle time to complete a process or lead time to serve a customer are all essential knowledge to progress with Lean Six Sigma. Appreciative Inquiry taught me the importance of using stories as an additional source of 'data'. Narrative is often ignored or dismissed when conducting process improvement, yet it has a huge potential to complement our analysis and 'fact finding'. Appreciative Inquiry also highlights the choice we have and the relevancy of stories about 'high moments' (of success, excellence or overcoming challenges) to driving change. Using narratives, and positive narratives in particular, is a useful addition to Lean and Six Sigma. Which is more engaging to listen to: a detailed report about the efforts to collect and validate data; an analysis of different data points on a chart; or a story of a particular, successful experience?

3 Simultaneity of inquiry and action

The practice of Six Sigma in particular places an emphasis on collecting data for analysis and sense-making before any action is taken, thus creating a (sometimes artificial) gap between inquiry and action. Although Lean Thinking doesn't necessarily separate inquiry and action in the same way, we often see improvement teams spending time analysing process maps or root causes before taking any improvement action. As was demonstrated in the story of the rail company in the previous chapter, inquiry often leads to paying attention to a certain direction of thinking and action. The questions we ask our colleagues and clients shift their attention and may lead them into taking an action in a specific direction. Our questions are followed by action and can be powerful! Let's use them wisely.

This case story and the three key points above demonstrate the value Appreciative Inquiry can have in process improvement. Let's explore what Solution Focus can add to the mix.

CASE STUDY Appreciative Inquiry
and process improvement – a case story

A recent conversation I held with a branch manager of a fast-growing Internet Service Provider in India demonstrates the value of Appreciative Inquiry in delivering improvements to business processes. Appreciative Inquiry pointed us to a different, more strength-based and 'whole' path towards improvement, a path that was not otherwise visible.

The Internet Service Provider in this story had been particularly successful in winning customers. Their customer base had grown from 5,000 to 150,000 over the short period of two years! I visited one of their branches and was introduced to the branch manager.

I was curious about the phenomenal rate of growth they enjoyed. I asked the branch manager what enabled this huge growth. What was working *so well* that made it all happen? The manager listed all the 'key success factors' – caller response rate, clear communication by customer service reps, consistent service levels and good technology. I asked for a story that explained the growth and again received lots of data and indicators.

The conversation went around in circles for a few minutes until I asked the branch manager to tell me about the best customer experience he personally remembered. Surprisingly, a story came out very easily! It was a great story about the long-winded journey of a customer who was keen on having an internet connection through this particular ISP. He went through all the departments in the company (including the branch manager)! Throughout his six-month long and winding journey, the customer and those interacting or serving him had to overcome many challenges until a working connection to the internet was established.

Another consultant who was with me at the meeting observed that throughout the story a key theme he had heard from the manager was around 'commitment to the customer'. The branch manager agreed that 'commitment' was indeed the most important contributor to his (and the branch's) success. He then followed on, without any prompting, to share an inspiring leadership story that showed his commitment to one of his employees.

The manager asked how he could apply the new insights around the value of commitment to his 'complaint resolution process' and to growing his subscriber base even further. I asked, 'What do you want to be committed to and what do you want your team to be committed to in that regard?' 'Resolving complaints quickly and reducing the ratio of complaints to customers' was his response. I asked what outcome would be even better. He responded 'having no complaints'. We continued the conversation a bit further, exploring what could be 'even better' and eventually landed on a different topic for inquiry – 'perfect connections'. This topic was applicable on multiple levels:

1 The technical level (or process) of connecting a customer to the internet.

2 Customers' interactions with service representatives and their experiences of going through multiple relevant business processes.

3 Internal conversations the service representatives held with the technical or billing teams, and the process of installing or fixing a connection.

4 Finally, it also applied to conversations between employees and managers, and internal management processes.

Naturally, having (or raising the level of) 'perfect connections' would cover the concerns around complaints and then some. What an inspiring topic!

Once we had a topic in mind, I suggested we follow by inquiring about and mapping the multiple processes around the above types of 'perfect connections'. What enables the company to successfully connect a customer to the internet without delay? What exactly happens when a customer is experiencing a 'perfect connection' with a service representative over the phone? How does the service representative form 'perfect connections' with other departments involved in delivering a service? What would make them even better or more frequent?

Solution Focus

Solution Focus introduced me to three guiding principles of change that greatly influenced my practice of process improvement:

1 Don't fix what isn't broken

Who decides what is 'broken'? The fact that a leadership team, a process owner, an influential stakeholder or even the end customer thinks that a process is 'broken' or inefficient and therefore needs to be improved is only a starting point. What do others who touch the process think? If they don't think that the process is broken or that it requires an improvement, you will be facing a very difficult task in trying to drive a change. Creating a 'platform for change' by engaging everyone involved around a shared definition of what is actually wanted, what the situation will be with the problem solved and what the benefit is of getting there, is a much better start.

2 Find what works and do more of it

Every situation is different, no matter how similar it may seem to other situations we have faced before, a story we read about or a problem that was solved in another organization. We often seek the 'magic tool' – a tool that was hailed by 'experts' and that has proven to be useful in other organizations. Finding what works requires us to focus our attention: to look for and inquire into what works in the situation in front of us. If you or someone external to a process 'knows' what *should* work, then you will undoubtedly try to find supporting evidence, and therefore miss important clues to what *really* works. Not knowing what should be done and staying curious about finding clues is the easiest way to see the way forward more clearly. Many of the Solution Focus tools are useful in the search for what is working and for finding ways to do more of it (for example, 'future perfect', 'counters' and 'affirmations' are useful in finding what works; 'scaling' and 'small steps' help uncover ways to do more of it). All the solution-focus tools can easily be integrated into process improvement through Lean Thinking and Six Sigma. What is important is not the tools: it's the mindset.

3 Make things as simple as possible, but not simpler (Albert Einstein)

The practice of Solution Focus highlights the value of simplicity in many ways:

- Using simple language – describing ideas, situations and the way forward using '$5 words instead of $5,000 words' – is helpful to successful change. (I chuckle as I think of the frequent use of Japanese words in Lean Thinking or the complex statistical terms in Six Sigma – clearly they are only 'simple' to those who are fluent in Japanese or are expert statisticians.)

- Making use of what is available instead of focusing on what isn't. Anything that seems to be connected with things working, going better, or even going less badly than normal, are worth exploring. This includes personal strengths, positive qualities, useful experiences, skills and cooperation as well as examples of the 'solution' happening already.

- Finding and taking the smallest, simplest step forward can be a great way to shift the situation and start a movement towards a better future. Small steps also offer fresh clues about what works. Improvement doesn't always require a complex project and months of analysis and planning.

CASE STUDY Solution Focus and process improvement

The following case story highlights the value of asking a few Solution Focus questions to generate fresh insights and the energy to implement them. The fact that the Solution Focus experience followed an evaluation of the business process from a deficit point of view further emphasizes the impact Solution Focus offers for process improvement.

The story

The client, a multinational with offices across Europe, was interested in improving the order-management process across several countries. Order management included all the activities taking place from the moment a customer ordered a product through to delivery, including invoicing, payment and service evaluation.

To start with, we agreed to visit the markets and conduct an evaluation of the current state of the process in order to identify the needs, current issues and potential future improvements in each market. For that purpose, we created a list of standard evaluation questions. The first market we decided to hold an evaluation for was Spain. The plan was to meet local staff and dedicate the first day to mapping all the relevant processes, identifying the current issues and collecting relevant data.

We started the evaluation by getting an overview of the market and its unique challenges, provided by the local team. We then went through our pre-defined evaluation questions. The next step was mapping the relevant processes and issues. This step took most of the day. At the end of the day, and as part of the standard questionnaire we had prepared, we asked the team what they thought we should focus on, and which improvements they would like to see in the process. We were surprised to hear their answers:

'We're already working on a couple of projects that would solve all our problems.'

'We do not really need any help from you.'

'Perhaps other markets could use your help better.'

'We're already implementing some of the ideas we shared with you.'

The work day was nearing its end, and it had been quite an exhausting exercise, so we concluded the evaluation at that stage. Both my colleague and I were disappointed by the final answers we had received and the apparent lack of engagement or appetite for our help.

The next day, I suggested meeting again with some members of the local team to ask them a few Solution Focus questions. Sitting with two local team members, I thanked them for everything they shared with us previously and explained that I had a few more questions. I told them that these additional questions were 'slightly different from the ones they had been asked before'. I did not elaborate. Due to the lack of interest at the end of the previous day, I felt that establishing a 'platform for change' (a Solution Focus term) would be beneficial. I therefore posed the following question:

> If, by some magic, you could have an additional day every week (ie a sixth working day out of a week of eight days – so not at the expense of your weekend) to be dedicated for process improvements only, what would you do with all that extra time? What would make the extra time worthwhile for you?

Immediately, I noticed a change in body language. Almost instantly, they became more relaxed and even smiled at me. It was clear they enjoyed being asked a 'different' question.

What followed was a very detailed response for over 15 minutes, helped by me occasionally asking 'what else?' The responses were rich in substance and language, raising new ideas for improvements they wanted to see and were prepared to pursue. These ideas ranged from relatively simple ones (eg finding a better way to sort paperwork), all the way to negotiating and implementing improved delivery service.

I added a second question:

> If I was part of the top management sitting at the head office, what would make it worthwhile for me and the company to create this extra day for you?

In response to the second question, they were able to justify the investment of time and resources by the impact it would have on employee morale, capabilities and quality of service.

I was also positively surprised by the answer they gave to a scaling question: 'On a scale from 1–10, where 10 is the detailed view of the possible future, where are you now?' It ranged from 6 to 7.5 out of 10. They finally agreed it was 6.5! I was genuinely surprised by the high rating they gave, especially following the experiences from the day before. I mentioned it to them and said 'Wow, so many good things are already in place, can you tell me more about what's making it 6.5 and not lower?' Their response again was very detailed and rich.

They felt confident that the next step of improvement would easily bring them to a rating of 8 or 9, and they were very clear about how they would get there. I asked a final 'resource' question: 'Can you give me examples of when the order-management process worked really well?' Again, it was answered very enthusiastically.

At the end of our conversation, both the local team members and I were excited. They felt confident about their current capabilities and commented positively on the 'different questions' I used. They were pleased with the new ideas that had emerged, and eager to take action. Coming out of the room, I shared my experience with my colleague who had not been in the room during the conversation. She was positively surprised with the outcome and asked me to integrate these 'new' questions in the market evaluation that followed!

We had a similar experience in Italy, where fresh insights emerged. In addition, members of the team kept a high level of engagement with us after we left their offices and continued to ask for our support with several improvement ideas. This was particularly encouraging, considering the obvious lack of interest in our improvement initiative at the end of the first day.

Can you see how some of the key principles behind Solution Focus and my experience with it offer added value to process improvement? What about the last approach, Positive Deviance, and its unique aspects?

Positive Deviance

In every community or organization, there are a few individuals or groups who have overcome or prevented the problem we wish to solve. Positive Deviance has its roots in the Positive Organizational Scholarship (POS) discipline. Although the practice of Positive Deviance to date has primarily focused on community development, we can expand this to cover operational processes as well. If we look at any process, we can find individuals or parts of the process already operating at a significantly better level than others. We can also find times when the process has yielded better results than normal. All of these, however uncommon they may be, are useful clues for the way forward if we wish to improve the process.

Some of the key points of Positive Deviance that are most relevant to process improvement are:

1   The system (all those involved with a given business process) should own the inquiry about the existence of positive deviants (unusually good results that are achieved *somehow*), understand what works and design ways to expand these practices. They will always be able to do a better job than external 'gurus', internal process 'experts' (such as Lean masters or people with colourful belts) or 'top management'.

2   It is better for the system to create its own benchmarks and monitor progress. Benchmarks are based on what the system wants to achieve once an area for inquiry or new ideas/designs for solutions are identified. External benchmarks or setting expectations from the top are less useful.

3   Positive Deviance process facilitation is based on deep respect for the system we work with, its members and its culture. It focuses on interactive engagement, and values the capacity of the community to take the lead – this is aligned with the original teachings of Lean Thinking and is worth keeping in mind every time we approach a new process-improvement project.

CASE STUDY   Positive Deviance
and process improvement – a case story

A separate conversation with the branch manager of the ISP mentioned earlier in this chapter demonstrates the use of Positive Deviance in improving business processes. In the situation described here, a simple dialogue containing a series of Positive Deviance questions provided useful insights enabling a solution to an efficiency problem. Even though other approaches have been tried, these insights had not surfaced before.

The story

The branch manager asked for my advice on how to improve the payment collection process in one of the areas of the city he was in charge of (let's call it area X). He explained that payments for internet services were collected by visiting each and every subscriber once a month, rather than online payments or through credit cards, direct debits or sending a cheque. The team responsible for the area was simply underperforming. Their target was 400 collections per team member each week. Can you imagine visiting 400 properties every week to collect payments?

I asked the manager if the process worked well elsewhere in his territory. He said that yes, in area Y, his collectors were very efficient. I asked what could be learned from that area that would apply to area X. The branch manager responded that they had already tried to transfer the 'best practices' from area Y back to area X, and that the situation had not improved much. He provided a variety of reasons why it didn't work (primarily because of the different geography and density of subscribers).

I then asked if there was anyone in the team serving area X who was already operating at, or close to, the desired level of performance. This seemed to generate more reflection and a few new ideas. It turned out that two members of the team were actually performing at a good level.

My third and final question was around those who were deemed not to perform well. I asked the manager if any of the underperforming team members had previously experienced a period of higher level of performance. Was there a particular week when one of them had performed well? Were there certain days of the week when they were able to perform particularly well? These questions seemed to create another breakthrough with my branch manager: he started coming up with lots of ideas and questions he wanted to ask the team members. Suddenly the way forward was more clear...

Just like Appreciative Inquiry and Solution Focus, Positive Deviance thinking and practice offers further expansion possibilities to the practice of Lean Six Sigma. New lines of potential inquiry, fresh insights and deep respect for the systems we work with are all very promising and within reach using this approach.

Summary

The case stories, as well as the deeper overview of the principles and key teachings behind these strength-based approaches, demonstrate how each approach offers a unique insight and flexible way to approach process improvement initiatives, as well as to engage with staff.

Now that you understand better what Appreciative Inquiry, Solution Focus and Positive Deviance thinking and practice offer to process-improvement initiatives, here are a few questions for you to reflect on:

1 Is it possible to reduce or even eliminate your performance problems by focusing on success?

2 How much emphasis do you place on quantitative data collection? Could stories inform you of existing wisdom and insights to tap into?

3 What is the essence of your success? What enables your organizational processes to perform well? Is it 'key success factors' such as technology, know-how or price competitiveness, or is it positive human interactions? What do you need to inquire into in order to generate greater success?

4 How do good processes and positive, useful and productive conversations interlink in your organization? Do you focus on the process and ignore the human interactions around it?

5 When you want to improve a particular process, where do you start and what are you seeking to understand in depth? Do you focus on analysing the underperforming parts or do you focus on the better-performing parts?

6 Which route of analysis could give you more useful ideas for actions you could take?

7 Which analysis would encourage the employees involved to contribute their time, energy and wisdom towards improvement?

The ideas in this chapter form the foundations of Strength-based Lean Six Sigma. They are the 'positive core' I discovered as I developed my thinking. In the next chapter I will define the topic in more detail using some of the concepts covered in this chapter, and highlight why it is important for you to consider it.

The principles behind the strength-based approach to Lean Six Sigma

In order to best understand the foundations of the strength-based approach to Lean Six Sigma and how to apply the thinking, we need to understand how the principles interact. To get there, let's take a step back to the underlying principles behind each one of these methodologies.

First, let's explore the principles behind Lean and Six Sigma. These principles were adapted from Womack and Jones.

There are five overriding principles to Lean:

1 Specify value from the point of view of the customer. The starting point is to recognize that only a small fraction of the total time, effort and resources spent in any organization actually adds value to the end customer.

2 Identify and map the value stream. The 'value stream' is the entire set of activities across all parts of the organization involved in jointly delivering a product or a service to the end customer. Eliminate, when possible, those steps that do not create value.

3 Create flow. Ensure that your product or service 'flows' to the customer without any interruption, detour or waiting.

4 Respond to customer pull. Gain an understanding of the customer demand on your product or service and then create a process to respond to this pull. This way, you produce only *what* the customer (or the next chain in the value stream) wants *when* it is wanted.

5 Pursue perfection. The gains from Lean Thinking become truly significant as all the steps above link together. As this happens, more and more layers of waste become visible and improvement continues towards the theoretical end point of perfection, where every asset and every action adds value for the end customer.

In following these five principles of Lean, we aim to implement a culture in which everyone in the organization is consistently delivering value to the customer. The actual process of implementing these principles involves a significant culture change at every level of the organization. Hopefully, this culture change enables the organization to maintain its high level of service and continuously improve over time.

Similarly, Six Sigma is a structured improvement methodology specifically focusing on reducing operational process variability as well as minimizing or eliminating defects in products and services. It is a set of analytical tools and methodologies used to understand the sources of process variability and defects, to analyse and identify root causes, and to implement the solutions and monitor the outcomes. Six Sigma's strength lies in its structured, methodical approach to problem solving (for example, the DMAIC process). It also focuses on understanding patterns in data and performing deep analysis.

Six Sigma is based on the following principles:

1 $Y = f(Xs) + a$: All outcomes and results (Y) are determined by inputs (Xs) with some degree of uncertainty (a). To change or improve the results (Y), you have to focus on the inputs (Xs), modifying and controlling them.

2 Only a critical few inputs (Xs) have significant effect on the output (Y). Concentrate on the critical few.

3 Variation is everywhere, and it degrades consistent, good performance (or as Jack Welch, the well known ex-General Electric CEO is often quoted as saying, 'Variation is evil'). The top priority for all Six Sigma practitioners is to identify where variation occurs, understand its root causes and minimize them.

4 Valid measurements and data are required foundations for consistent, breakthrough improvement.

The overall mission for Six Sigma practitioners is essentially the pursuit of process stability and consistent results that meet the customers' requirements.

Lean Six Sigma is an amalgamation of both Lean Thinking and Six Sigma and as such has adopted the principles of both. This allows the practitioner to choose which tools and analytical processes from the combined toolbox are most relevant to each situation.

How have these principles shaped Lean Six Sigma practice and tools?

All the tools within the Lean tool box (eg Value-Stream Map, 5S, Spaghetti Charts, Single Minute Exchange of Dies, Seven Wastes, Kanban, Poka Yoke and many others) are specifically designed to bring the Lean principles to life *in a given context or problem setting*. It is important to notice that almost all the tools and the questions we ask when we use these tools, or when we train people in the organization in Lean, share a common deficit-based focus. In other words, when we chart a Value-Stream Map, we often pay most attention to the wasteful and inefficient parts, trying our best to understand their sources and identify ways to eliminate them. When we use Spaghetti Charts, we are immediately drawn to excessive transport and movement. Very rarely do we look at the value-creating parts of our mapped processes or study them at length. We also never spare a second look at where in the Spaghetti Chart we already have cases of minimal travel or movement, nor do we ask what enabled these parts. The same goes for bottlenecks and most of the other tools or thinking processes in Lean – all turn the spotlight on the weakest parts of our organizational processes.

Similarly, in the practice of Six Sigma, we focus all of our attention on identifying defects (negative deviants from the expected performance) and unstable processes (processes with high or unpredictable variation). Our direction of analysis focuses on understanding the root causes of these defects and variations.

However, if we take a step back from these tools to look at the Lean and Six Sigma principles and at the mission statement for Six Sigma, we can see that they are stated from *a positive point of view*. All clearly describe what is desirable (ie what we wish to see more of) rather than what is undesirable (and therefore needs to be eliminated or reduced). The aspiration to improve – value to customers, flow, response to customer pull, perfection, stability and consistency – is absolutely essential and there is nothing wrong with it. It is only the common practice of these principles that actively guides us to make the deficit-focus our 'highway' towards bringing these principles to life. As a result, the strength-focus, which in my view can generate just as many transformational insights, becomes a lost 'dirt track' that nobody dares travel on.

Introducing the Appreciative Inquiry principles

Now that we have considered the principles underlining Lean Thinking and those underlining Six Sigma, it is a good idea to introduce the principles behind Appreciative Inquiry:

Appreciative Inquiry has six key principles:

1 **The Constructionist principle.** The Constructionist principle key messages are: reality is co-created with every conversation we have (words create worlds); every question we ask generates material that influences our understanding of reality; as a result, multiple realities may co-exist.

2 **The Simultaneity principle.** Our questions immediately influence the direction of thinking, conversation, understandings, beliefs and actions. Every question we pose is an intervention. When we understand and accept this, we understand that every such intervention ought to be thought through. Our choice of inquiry is fateful in that it launches new 'trains of thought' and influences the future we create. Our questions and reflections impact the system almost immediately after the question is introduced.

3 **The Poetic principle.** This principle states that individuals, teams and organizations are like endless books of stories and experiences to learn from and build upon. These stories can be told about every aspect of their experiences. Our choice of what to pay attention to in these stories determines what the outcome may be. In other words, our choices in each situation determine what we find. In addition, this principle invites us to think about what we want to see *more of*, or where we wish to head *towards*, rather than what we want to *reduce or move away from*.

4 **The Anticipatory principle.** The Anticipatory principle states that individuals and organizations change in the direction of their images of the future. These images influence our beliefs about what is possible for us in the future, and these beliefs in turn influence the actions we take and the future that unfolds. The more people share the same images of the future, the greater the chance to change in that direction. This means that the best way forward for an organization is to create and share as detailed an image as possible of its desired future.

5 **The Positive principle.** This principle challenges us to focus on what is positive and alive when we, our teams and our organizations are at their best. Every change effort requires a lot of energy to support it. Inquiring into our exceptional achievements in the past, what is strong in the present and our hopes for the best of the future, generates and releases this energy. We also choose to focus on the positive for another reason. As we learn from the Anticipatory principle, we and our organizations grow in the direction of our questions and our thoughts about the future. In order to unleash the potential for positive change, we choose to focus on the positive within us. Finally, the Positive principle highlights the choice we *always have* with regard to what we inquire into: if we inquire into our lowest moments, fears and failures, we are more likely to generate more of them in the future.

6 **The Wholeness principle.** This is an overarching principle when working with Appreciative Inquiry. Focusing on the whole system and bringing it into the conversation helps bring a variety of stories and possibilities. More stories and possibilities take us to, and stretch us beyond, our system's perceived potential. Involving everyone who is relevant to our learning and change activities in our inquiry, dreams, designs and delivery builds the organization's capacity for learning, growth and change. It also honours the multitude of opinions, perceptions, knowledge and experiences that exist within our organizations. This helps create a shared identity and direction for our future. The principle of Wholeness also invites us to look at each individual (whether ourselves or our colleagues) as whole beings. Each and every one of us is a whole human being bringing a whole life story and endless resourcefulness that can be useful to the change we drive.

Lean Six Sigma principles guide us towards the best, most efficient operational set up and functionality. Appreciative Inquiry principles are there to guide us towards creating a positive organizational change.

What do the Appreciative Inquiry principles mean in the context of Lean Six Sigma?

How can we connect and combine them?

1 **The Poetic and Positive principles.** We have a choice of what we inquire into. Inquiring into the positive can be very powerful in driving change. *What we ask determines what we 'find'.*

2 **The Constructionist and Simultaneity principles.** These principles state that reality isn't external to our views or our conversations (ie objective) but is always influenced by them. Therefore, asking questions and seeking out data affects what we find rather than merely aiding us in collecting data for analysis and later action. *What we find determines how we talk.*

3 The Anticipatory principle. The image we have about the future affects the direction of our present actions. *How we talk determines how we 'see' our future. How we 'see' our future determines what we achieve!*

If we take the Appreciative Inquiry principles into consideration when looking at the activities taking place during a typical process-improvement project or a workshop, it becomes obvious that we may actually set ourselves up for failure. If we only seek out where the process is broken, how to eliminate waste, remove bottlenecks or inquire into defects (negative deviants from normal performance), we magnify the problems. The sheer nature of the questions we ask (for example, 'Where is the waste?', 'What isn't working?', 'Why is the process stuck?', 'What are the root causes of this defect?' etc) and the conversations we have with the people involved in the process influence the way people see the reality of the process and other work they are involved with. As a result, new waste and bottlenecks may actually be created and more problems emerge!

So, do I advocate ignoring current wastes, defects and bottlenecks in the process? No, far from it! What I suggest is approaching them from a different direction. I simply assume that in every process, something works well and look for ways to enhance it.

Another way of looking at it is summarized in Figure 5.1:

FIGURE 5.1 Different directions to achieve the desired Lean outcomes

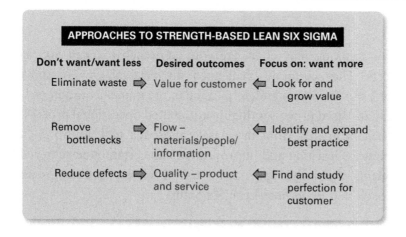

In this chart, we see that the classic Lean Six Sigma approach and the Strength-based Lean Six Sigma approach share the same desired outcomes. It is only the focus of inquiry that is different. This difference is fateful.

Similarly Figure 5.2 below highlights the different paths available to us in driving continuous learning and improvement.

FIGURE 5.2 Different approaches to achieving continuous learning and improvement

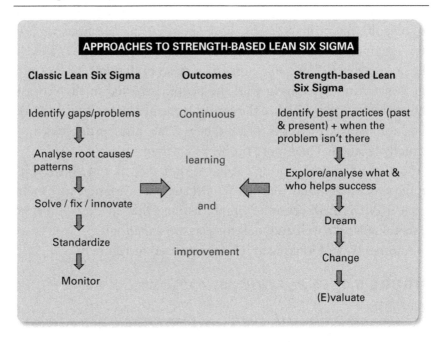

This thinking may challenge your approach to Lean Six Sigma projects. They certainly challenged my original way of thinking about Lean Six Sigma and, in particular, the implementation of Lean in human-based processes (highly automated operational process can still benefit greatly from the classic approach to Lean Six Sigma). Continuous learning and improvement can certainly be achieved by following alternative approaches to the classic 'problem-focused' approach that underlines Lean Six Sigma.

Additional principles to consider from Solution Focus and Positive Deviance, and their meaning for Lean Six Sigma

So far, I have focused on the principles of Appreciative Inquiry and the impact they make on the thinking and practice of Lean Six Sigma. In this section, I will explore some of the Solution Focus and Positive Deviance principles that I believe add additional insights. This is not the complete selection of the principles of these two approaches (as detailed in Chapter 2), but rather the ones that in my view complement the Appreciative Inquiry principles I have already explored above, and the ones that may bring the biggest benefits to the classic practice of Lean Six Sigma.

Selected Solution Focus and Positive Deviance principles:

1 Change is happening all the time. Our job is to identify and amplify *useful change*.

2 There is no one 'right' way of looking at things: different views may fit the facts equally well.

3 Detailed understanding of the 'problem' is usually of little help in arriving at the solution. The direct route to problem solving lies in identifying what is going on when the problem does not happen.

4 Members of the system recognize that 'someone just like me' can get results, even in the worst case scenarios (evidence from within).

5 The system creates its own benchmarks and monitors progress.

These additional principles can expand the thinking and practice of Lean Six Sigma in several ways. For example, the implication of the first principle when applied to the 'Control' stage of the DMAIC cycle is almost a complete reinvention and a total shift in focus. Rather than focusing our attention on stabilizing – setting in stone the change we implemented – we should continue the learning and identification of new and emerging positive change.

The third principle essentially means that all our efforts during the 'Measure' and 'Analyse' stages to find the root causes for failures and wastes do not form the most direct route towards solutions.

When we adopt the fourth principle ('people like me can get results'), we are inviting the internal knowledge that resides within the system. This sometimes means a significant shift from a prevalent mindset that hopes for ideas for improvement and solutions to come from external experts and 'best practices'.

Finally, the fifth principle introduces another area for growth in the practice of process improvement. Are we ready to let benchmarks and progress monitoring be fully owned by the systems we work with rather than have them be set and monitored from the outside?

Summary

David Cooperrider, who co-created the Appreciative Inquiry methodology, states that 'a constructionist would argue that the seeds of organizational change are implicit in the first questions asked. The questions asked become the material out of which the future is conceived and constructed.'

As already indicated, the common practice of taking the deficit-inquiry line in order to improve processes ('the deficit highway') is only a choice. We can always choose differently. How about taking the (currently) less-used 'dirt track' of strengths as mentioned earlier and turning it into the new 'yellow brick road' of Lean Six Sigma?

By following a more positive and affirming line of questioning we can use the answers to create a more robust process and in an indirect way reduce or eliminate the waste more naturally as operators and managers orientate themselves towards the better parts of the process. In fact, our effort to seek what is value-generating for the customer in a given process (rather than what is wasting value) will drive the people participating in the exercise to consciously or unconsciously seek ways to deliver even more value to customers. Finally, this line of inquiry and learning completely bypasses the natural suspicion employees have towards any efforts to 'lean processes'. It will ensure wider support with longer lasting impact and will yield better outcomes for all.

The same goes for Six Sigma. Finding out where we have positive deviants, what enables them and what is keeping our processes stable and predictive can be a powerful line of inquiry.

I hope that this chapter gave you enough material to think about, and possibly a few useful ideas to try in your next improvement workshop. Imagine what would happen during an improvement workshop or a project if you asked different questions such as:

1 When has this process worked well? Can you tell me what was happening then?

2 What has been the best outcome of this process? What made it possible?

3 What do you like most about this process? When have you been most proud about your work here?

4 What is working well today? Where and when does this process deliver value to customers?

5 Where in the process are parts flowing well?

6 If you had the ability to improve this process as you wish, what would you improve first? How would the process look then? What would be different?

The next chapter will provide you with several routes for exploring your positive core in order to help you innovate and create your own way of working with Strength-based Lean Six Sigma.

Exploring the 'positive core'

06

My knowledge of Strength-based Lean Six Sigma and appreciation of the substantial benefits it can bring to the practice of process improvement were developed out of my 'positive core' of knowledge and experience. This chapter will help you understand your own journey and thinking so that you can gain a clear view of your 'positive core'. This, in turn, will guide you in paving your path forward.

Exploring and making sense of the 'positive core' is an important step when working with Appreciative Inquiry. It enables us to move from where we are now to where we hope to be in the future. The positive core is everything we know that is at the heart of our successes to date, all that is truly essential to our current situation and is available to us as we imagine and build our future. Keeping and building on the positive core ensures continuity of the past as we move confidently into the future, thus raising the chances of future success. The positive core is essentially the 'seed' of future growth and development.

Just as each plant produces its own seeds, the positive core is context dependent; in each situation and with each individual the positive core is unique. The more we understand our own positive core and the positive core of the organization we work with, the higher the chance that we can be at our best and serve our organizations better. It also enables us as change agents to create our own unique way of approaching and inspiring change in the systems we work with. You may start practising some of the ideas and tools I present in this book but ultimately your way of practising Strength-based Lean Six Sigma may be different from my way (or the way presented in this book). Ideally, it should be based on your unique positive core.

This chapter offers several questions to enable you to explore and identify your own unique positive core. These questions may also be useful as you interact with others in your system. The questions are organized in the following categories:

1 Exploring the best of Lean Six Sigma as you know and understand it.

2 Exploring the best of Appreciative Inquiry, Solution Focus and Positive Deviance.

3 Exploring the best in yourself as a change agent or an improvement practitioner.

4 Exploring the best in the system(s) you're working with.

5 Exploring your hopes for the future.

Throughout this chapter, I will share some of my own experiences and insights as examples of my own positive core. Please start with the questions that are most relevant to you, or the ones that intrigue you the most. Keep a record of the ideas that emerge for you.

Exploring the best of Lean Six Sigma

I was first introduced to Six Sigma through a 'Green Belt' training programme. I then proceeded to work with and support others with several successful projects to improve sales-force effectiveness. It gave me unique insights, particularly because at the time very little was known or available about the use of Six Sigma outside of manufacturing. One insight I gained was the importance of using simpler language to explain the key concepts and tools. I also learned that it was almost irrelevant to strive to a Six Sigma quality level when working on sales processes as they were dependent on human interactions and hard to 'control'. I learned that each cycle of discovery through Six Sigma led to another cycle of learning and expansion elsewhere.

I later gained a qualification as a Black Belt and then a Master Black Belt, which provided me the opportunity to train others and to work on larger, more complex projects. A few years later, I was also trained in Lean Thinking tools, in particular facilitating Kaizen events. Several concepts were already familiar from my previous experience, so it felt comfortable to adopt Lean in addition to Six Sigma. From that point I enjoyed facilitating many Kaizen events, delivering substantial impact. I also appreciated the opportunities I had to train others and to affect the organizational culture in a positive way.

Looking back, I particularly appreciated the methodical approach to problem solving, the thinking frameworks, the aspiration to continuously improve the way business was done and the in-depth insights each project provided. I had my favourite tools (process mapping, SIPOC, Voice of the Customer, the Seven Wastes, root cause analysis and regressions). These favourite tools served me well over time in many different situations.

The positive core of Lean Six Sigma as I experienced it:

1 The drive for continuous improvement, raising quality levels, flow and value to customer – all are very positive and inspiring goals.

2 The emphasis given to studying reality 'as it is' rather than 'as it should be'.

3 Continuous learning and spreading knowledge to wider populations.

4 How visible the positive impact of Lean activities can be.

5 Making a positive impact on business results and customers' experiences.

6 The methodical approach and thinking structure Six Sigma offers through DMAIC.

7 Process or value-stream mapping.

8 Raising interesting and often unexpected insights about organizational processes.

9 Bringing clarity through visual management and useful metrics.

Let's explore your own Lean Thinking and Six Sigma positive core. The following questions are meant to provide a few starting points, possibly raising new and different questions for you:

1 Think back to the first time you heard about Six Sigma or Lean Thinking (or even the combination – Lean Six Sigma):

- What was the situation?
- Who was telling you about it?
- What was most intriguing or interesting to you about it?
- How did others around you (your peers, your manager, people who reported to you or your clients) react to it? What were they impressed by?
- What prompted the person who told you about it to mention it?

2 How did you continue your learning journey and deepen your understanding of Lean Six Sigma? It may be that you followed a well-defined certification journey or a more organic, self-defined learning through reading and experimentation.

- What worked particularly well?
- What learning experiences stand out to you? In what way?

3 Now, reflect about your best Lean or Six Sigma experience to date. It may have been a long time in the past or more recent.

- What was the situation?
- What was your role?
- Who else was involved?
- What was so good about that experience? What made it stand out for you?
- What capabilities and strengths did you discover you had?
- Which tools, thinking processes or ways of practising Lean Six Sigma did you choose to use? What insights did they provide?
- How did you implement the change and what impact did you achieve?

- With the wisdom of hindsight, what do you wish you could have done at the time, to make that experience even better?

4 What other great experiences did you have with Lean and Six Sigma? What makes these experiences stand out for you?

5 What is the best article or book you have read or the best story you have heard regarding Lean Six Sigma?

6 What meaningful interactions or conversations have you held around Six Sigma or Lean Thinking?

7 What did others you have worked with particularly appreciate about the way you practise or teach Lean Thinking or Six Sigma?

8 Which tool(s) do you find most useful? What makes them so useful?

9 What worked best for the organizations or systems you worked with while practising Lean or Six Sigma?

10 Time has passed since you started working with Lean and Six Sigma; what do you now know about it that is important to keep in mind for the future?

11 What do you particularly value about Lean or Six Sigma? What, in your view, is unique and useful about them?

12 How has knowing about or practising Lean or Six Sigma served you particularly well? What benefits did you gain?

13 If you were to change the way you (or others around you) practise Lean Thinking or Six Sigma, what changes would you seek?

14 Imagine you were given the opportunity to create the next generation of Lean Thinking or Six Sigma, a new approach that will become well-known and widely practised in a few years. What would the new approach include or how would it be practised? What would give you the confidence that this approach is better and innovative? How would others notice? What would be different? What else?

Having answered some or all of these questions (or other questions that have emerged while reading these) what themes are emerging?

What is the positive core of your Lean Thinking or Six Sigma experience, practice and knowledge? Draw a 'mind map', a diagram or find another creative way to express and capture this positive core.

Exploring the best of Appreciative Inquiry, Solution Focus and Positive Deviance

In Chapter 3, 'The Birth of Strength-based Lean Six Sigma', I described how I learned about both Appreciative Inquiry and Solution Focus. I learned about Positive Deviance through a conversation with a highly regarded and experienced Six Sigma consultant. All of these strength-based approaches share key ideas, although the way they are practised is unique to each approach. I was instantly attracted to the positive direction all of these approaches had. I also liked the energizing experience of both asking and answering strength-based questions. Finally, the creativity that both I and others I worked with were able to release at the 'Dream' stage of Appreciative Inquiry regularly surprised and excited me.

The positive core of Appreciative Inquiry, Solution Focus and Positive Deviance as I experienced it:

1 The power of the Appreciative Inquiry principles, which together form a complete path to creating positive 'whole-system' change for individuals, teams, organizations or even very large systems.

2 The gift one gives and receives by asking and responding to appreciative, strength-based, questions.

3 The energy and creativity unleashed through the Appreciative Inquiry process.

4 The various Appreciative Inquiry models, tools and case stories available, and the willingness of Appreciative Inquiry practitioners to share their learning and knowledge.

5 The powerful Solution Focus tools – the impact and incredible insights they offer while staying very simple and flexible to practise.

6 Social construction – learning that reality is constantly defined and redefined through conversations with ourselves and others, and through the stories we share.

7 Reframing the starting points for inquiry and exploration from what we want to reduce, solve or move away from to what we want to see more of.

8 While I enjoyed being an 'expert' in Lean and Six Sigma, Appreciative Inquiry, Solution Focus and Positive Deviance all freed me from being 'an expert' by showing me how those I work with are the real experts in their work and their lives, and that they already have the knowledge they need to be able to move forward.

9 The level of engagement and commitment generated through experiencing these approaches without having to 'encourage', persuade or 'sell' them.

What do you already know or have you already experienced about strength-based approaches to change? Here are a few questions to help you explore your own strength-based positive core. They may raise new and different questions for you:

1 Think back to the first time you heard about strength-based change or any of the strength-based approaches I refer to in this book (primarily Appreciative Inquiry, Solution Focus or Positive Deviance although if you know or use other approaches, please consider them too).

– What was the situation?

– Who was telling you about it?

– What was most intriguing or interesting to you about it? What were you impressed by?

– Did the first exposure you had include an actual experience of these approaches, however short or long? If so, what stood out for you?

2 How did you continue your learning journey and deepen your understanding of these approaches? You may have attended a workshop or read an article or a book or found other useful resources.

- What worked particularly well?
- What learning experiences stand out to you? In what way?

3 Now, reflect about your best Appreciative Inquiry, Solution Focus or Positive Deviance experience to date. The experience may have been a long time in the past or more recent.

- What was the situation?
- What was your part?
- Who else was involved?
- What was particularly good about that experience? What made it stand out for you?
- What capabilities and strengths did you discover you had through this experience?
- What tools or unique and impactful questions did you choose to use? What insights did they provide?
- What unfolded next?
- With the wisdom of hindsight, what do you wish you could have done at the time to make that experience even better?

4 What other excellent experiences did you have with Appreciative Inquiry, Solution Focus or Positive Deviance? What makes these experiences stand out for you?

5 What is the best or most inspiring story you have heard about these approaches?

6 What meaningful interactions or conversations have you held with other Appreciative Inquiry, Solution Focus or Positive Deviance practitioners?

7 What did others you have worked with particularly appreciate about the way you practise strength-based change?

8 Which tool(s) or questions are your favourites? Why?

9 What worked best for the individuals, teams, organizations or systems you have worked with on strength-based change intervention(s)?

10 Time has passed since you started working with Appreciative Inquiry, Solution Focus or Positive Deviance: what do you now know about these approaches that is important to keep in mind for the future?

11 What do you particularly value about Appreciative Inquiry, Solution Focus or Positive Deviance? What, in your view, is unique and useful about them?

12 How has knowing about or practising these approaches served you particularly well? What benefits have you gained?

13 If you were to change the way you (or others around you) practise strength-based approaches, what changes would you seek?

14 Imagine you were given the opportunity to create the next innovation in strength-based change, a new approach that will become well-known and widely practised in a few years. What would the new approach include or look like? How would you notice that this approach is better and innovative? How would others notice? What would be different? What else?

Having answered some or all of these questions (or other questions that have emerged while reading these questions) what connections can you see? What is the positive core of your experience, practice and knowledge of Appreciative Inquiry, Solution Focus or Positive Deviance? Draw a 'mind map', a diagram or find another creative way to express this positive core.

Exploring the best in yourself as a change agent/improvement practitioner

Realizing that I was a positive change agent who enjoys and finds immense satisfaction in helping individuals, teams and whole organizations change for the better was in itself a powerful insight for me. It also opened the door to a path for all that I have learned about various change practices and Strength-based Lean Six Sigma. I find change and the learning that is involved with it exciting, rewarding, intriguing and promising. Some of the change processes I went through were scary or involved high levels of uncertainty, but ultimately they took me and those around me to a better place. I believe that the fact you are reading this book probably indicates that you are also passionate about driving change.

What is so energizing in leading change? Here is my positive core as a change agent:

1 Inspiring or releasing new conversations, ideas and actions.

2 Posing the right question at the right time.

3 Staying unfazed by chaotic situations and being able to create a safe 'container' for others.

4 Looking for what is possible in every situation and what strengths can be built on with each individual or team.

5 Finding the positive in others and in each situation and reflecting it back to those I work with, thus raising their level of confidence, energy and hopes for the future.

6 Using creative thinking and powerful metaphors.

Now, let's explore your positive core as a change agent. Here are a few useful questions to reflect on:

1 If you are at present or were previously in a role that primarily involved driving change or improving and developing organizations (either internal to the organization or as an external consultant), how did you arrive at that position?

  – What personal development journey did you take to get there?

  – What were the high points of change?

  – What insights did you gain from the choices you made?

2 How did you develop and deepen your approach to leading change or improvement?

  – What frameworks, mental models, processes and ways of thinking did you learn about and adopt?

– What learning experiences about change stand out to you?
In what way?

3 Reflect on your best organizational change or improvement
experience to date. The experience may have been a long time
in the past or more recent.

– What was the situation?

– What was your role?

– Who else was involved?

– What was so good about that experience? What made it
stand out for you?

– What capabilities and strengths did you discover you had
through this experience?

– What tools, frameworks or approaches did you choose to
use? What insights did they provide to you and others?

– What unfolded next?

– With the wisdom of hindsight, what do you wish you
could have done at the time to make that experience even
better?

4 What other excellent change or improvement experiences
(both personally and at work) did you have? What makes
these experiences stand out for you?

5 What is the best or most inspiring story you have heard about
organizational change or improvement?

6 What meaningful interactions or conversations have you held
with other change leaders? What powerful insights did they
share?

7 What did others you have worked with particularly appreciate
about the way you drive change or improvement?

8 Which change approaches, frameworks or models are your
favourites? Why?

9 What worked best for the individuals, teams, organizations
or systems you worked with while delivering change or
improvement?

10 If you have been driving change and improvement for a while, what do you now know about it that is important to keep in mind for the future?

11 What do you particularly value about the way you think about change and the first actions you take? What, in your view, is unique and useful about them?

12 What are you most passionate about when you think of organizational change or improvement?

13 How has working with change or organizational improvement served you and others you know particularly well? What benefits did you gain?

14 If you were to change the way you (or others around you) respond to or work with change/improvement, what changes would you seek?

15 Imagine you just released a book covering the next innovation in driving change and/or delivering improvements. Your book is highly praised by leading practitioners and thought leaders in your profession. What is covered in your new book? How would you notice that your ideas and approaches are better and innovative? How would others notice? What would be different? What else?

Now that you have reflected on these or similar questions, what themes have appeared repeatedly? What is at the heart of your change or improvement experience, practice and knowledge of Appreciative Inquiry, Solution Focus or Positive Deviance? What metaphors or other creative expressions represent this positive core for you?

Exploring the best in the system(s) you are working with

This part is particularly important to readers who work for, or are part of, a system. Some of these questions can be used by consultants together with their clients to help the clients' situation.

Being able to identify the positive core of your organization, system or the situation you are facing is an excellent starting point to inspire change and deliver growth. It is a more natural stepping stone to the future than any artificially created 'burning platform' or leadership directive. You may also find new ideas for a better future in your organization.

Here are a few questions to help you think about your organization's positive core:

1 What drew you to work with this organization?

2 Think of a time when you experienced your organization at its best.

  - What was the situation?

  - What was your role?

  - Who else was involved?

  - What specifically made that experience the best?

  - What elements of that experience would you like to experience again or see growing in the future?

3 What is working well today? Even if the current situation seems challenging, something is probably still working well. What is it?

4 What do you particularly value about the organization and the people you work with or those who are part of it?

5 What strengths or advantages does the organization have both internally and externally (in the marketplace and with its external stakeholders)?

6 Suppose this organization was, by some sort of magic, able to overcome all its current challenges, what would be different? How would you notice that the situation was different? Who else would notice? What would make the change possible?

7 What three wishes do you have for the future of the organization?

What have these questions helped uncover for you? What useful insights did you gain that can help you in the future?

Exploring your hopes for the future

At this stage, my hope is that you have gained new and useful insights that you can use and integrate with everything you already know about your practice, your situation or your organization to imagine and be able to deliver growth or positive change. Here are a few final questions to help you reflect on it:

1 What key insights and themes have you discovered?

2 What do you now hope for yourself, your practice and your organization?

3 When is this hope either fully or partly present? What helps it?

4 What do you feel drawn to? What makes it particularly attractive?

5 What is the smallest step you can take to move forward? What might be smaller still?

6 And finally, as you think of all the themes you have unearthed, the mind maps or other creative representations you created, what will inform your own unique practice of Strength-based Lean Six Sigma? What would you like to try now?

Summary

This chapter was meant to take you deeper into your own positive core in your practice, knowledge and experience. As I mentioned before, understanding my positive core was instrumental in my own development and learning, and I am confident it will be in yours as well. In Appreciative Inquiry, it is also an essential connector between 'the best that is' and the 'best of what can be', the key objective of the 'Dream' stage. 'Dream' is my chosen title for the next part of the book, in which I will talk about how Strength-based Lean Six Sigma practice and processes look, its guiding characteristics and how performance metrics and scorecards can use a strength-based approach.

Before you move to the next part of the book, I invite you to reflect on and choose the topic you are most intrigued by. What would you like to expand your understanding of? The following questions may be useful:

1 What makes sense about everything I have read so far? What chimes well?

2 What do I now know about Strength-based Lean Six Sigma?

3 How can I understand it better?

4 What will it enable me to do or achieve? What is its promise?

5 In what ways can Strength-based Lean Six Sigma be useful or add value to everything I already know and do?

PART THREE
Dream

Appreciative Inquiry teaches us that keeping the continuity of the best of the past and building on the 'positive core' are the building blocks for the best in the future. In this part, I will use my findings about the positive core to chart a 'provocative proposition' (a term taken from Appreciative Inquiry) for a way forward that is full of new possibilities.

Chapter 7 begins the 'Dream' part of the book by describing the characteristics of Strength-based Lean Six Sigma – the combination of strength-based change and Lean Six Sigma – and highlights why we should consider it. Strength-based Lean Six Sigma is, of course, the key 'provocative proposition' of this book. Chapter 8 will talk about the key assumptions guiding the classic practice of Lean Six Sigma and offer alternative assumptions.

Chapter 9 explores in detail the common Lean Six Sigma thinking frameworks, suggesting a strength-based approach to all. I will follow these frameworks with a vision of how a strength-based approach can enrich the performance metrics and dashboards we use; and finally, I will close the Dream part with possible 'provocative propositions' that highlight how strength-based thinking can be used at a whole organization level, at a process or project level, with a project team or by simply applying the thinking at the tool level.

What is Strength-based Lean Six Sigma?

07

All approaches to change and improvement are essentially socially constructed and very dependent on the context and time in which they were developed and introduced. This is just as true of the Toyota Production System, originally developed as an ongoing system for solving challenges in production, as it is of all the quality and efficiency frameworks you may be familiar with. The attempt to summarize, standardize and transfer these approaches can sometimes reduce their effectiveness (as many of us who tried to implement Lean practices outside of Toyota, or Six Sigma practices outside of Motorola and GE, can testify).

The strength-based approach to Lean Six Sigma is no different. It is also socially constructed in this time and age, and in a particular context. Your practice and understanding of Strength-based Lean Six Sigma may differ, and that is fine. My hope is that you find some of the principles and thoughts I introduce in this book relevant in your context, and that you extend it further.

How do I define Strength-based Lean Six Sigma?

Strength-based Lean Six Sigma is a fresh approach to Lean Six Sigma through the lens of the leading approaches to strength-based change.

Rather than provide a 'watertight' definition for Strength-based Lean Six Sigma, I prefer to highlight the key characteristics of working with Lean Six Sigma from a strength-based approach. If you notice some of these characteristics in your work, you are already underway in applying a strength-based approach. If you're applying few or none of these characteristics, I invite you to consider and try integrating as many of them as you can into your practice.

The characteristics of Strength-based Lean Six Sigma are:

1 Using the great Lean Six Sigma tools many of us are familiar with and find useful, while applying a strengths approach. In other words, when you use Lean Six Sigma tools that you and your clients (internal or external) are comfortable with, while focusing on what is working well in the situation, what existing strengths and points of peak performance can be observed and what the client wants more of, you are heading in the direction of Strength-based Lean Six Sigma. In theory, this may sound easy to achieve; however, in practice, it may challenge us – the improvement practitioners – to extend our skills and comfort zones.

2 Expanding the existing dialogues in organizations (by inviting strengths, a focus on positive deviants and a search for excellence) to create the ability to see strengths, best practices and value as well as problems, waste and defects (thus significantly expanding the Lean guideline of 'go see').

3 Bringing a combined focus on the systems and the human sides. No longer do we over-emphasize one at the expense of the other. Also, a combined human- and system-focus is fully aligned with the teachings of Deming and the Toyota Production System.

4 Applying any or all of the principles of change from Appreciative Inquiry, Solution Focus and Positive Deviance in our practice of Lean Six Sigma – essentially building a bridge between the two paradigms of problem solving and strength-focus.

5 Working towards the desired Lean Six Sigma outcomes of quality, efficiency, flow and continuous improvement by using strength-based change principles. For more details about the principles, refer to Chapter 5.

6 Understanding that in every challenging area, something must be working well, which can therefore be used as the platform to create

the desired improvement. This also means that we predominantly rely on internal knowledge from within the system we work with, and that we accept that every situation, however similar it may be to past situations, is different. Every situation offers its own possibilities and requires its own inquiry.

7 Fundamentally changing the direction of our questions. Practitioners of classic Lean Six Sigma processes and tools normally ask fairly standard questions to guide them in focusing their efforts about how to proceed. These sets of questions and the assumptions underlying them radically change when we adopt the strength-based approach.

As you can see, these characteristics are intended to give you enough of a guideline to move in the right direction, yet they are deliberately left flexible enough for you to create your own way of applying Strength-based Lean Six Sigma, building on your own positive core. Chapter 6 provides guidance on how to explore and build on your positive core in more detail.

- Do you already apply some or all of these characteristics?
- Which one of them stands out for you, and is inviting you to explore or try it out?
- What, in your view, might be the benefit of applying your favourite characteristics from this list on your work, and on the people and organizations you're working with?

Why this combination?

My own experience, as well as experiences shared by other practitioners, highlights several different benefits of working with Lean Six Sigma from a strength-based approach. I chose to split these benefits into three categories:

1 Ensuring continuity of the best from the past.

2 Finding new resources and innovating new ideas ('the whole is greater than the sum of its parts').

TABLE 7.1 The many benefits of combining Lean Six Sigma and strength-based change

Category	Benefits
Continuity of the best from the past	• Honouring the best of the past instead of dismissing it. • Meeting clients 'where they are': If they are comfortable with and like Lean Six Sigma tools and thinking, we stay tuned to their strengths (from Lean Six Sigma)… and then introduce the strength-based approach.
'The whole is greater than the sum of its parts'	• Combining the two approaches can exceed either individually in problem-solving results (novel solutions, moving from 'good' to 'great'). • Lean Six Sigma and all strength-based approaches to change can be seen as improbable pairs or polarities. My experience has shown that finding practical ways to work with polarities is immensely valuable. • Lean Six Sigma and strength approaches to change are supplementary. There are benefits in combining them, including: combining the technical and human side of our systems; combining analytical and intuitive thinking; injecting creativity and energy into process improvements; uncovering and spreading tacit knowledge.
Easier transition to an improved future and sustained improvement	• It helps create momentum for change. • It drives wider and deeper engagement as well as more acceptance (in Lean this is called *Nemawashi*, that is consensus and involvement in decision making). • The strength-based approach to change can help create a sustained culture of continuous improvement. Such a culture has been particularly challenging to achieve even within the organizations that are most successful in applying Lean Six Sigma.

3 Easier transition to an improved future and sustained improvement.

Table 7.1 details the benefits from each category. Based on all these benefits, I truly believe that Strength-based Lean Six Sigma is the next step and can influence 'the future of Lean Six Sigma'.

What other benefits can you see to this approach?

Why not stick to either one approach or the other?

This question should be answered from two directions:

1 What does Strength-based Lean Six Sigma add to the practice of classic Lean Six Sigma?

2 What does the strength-based approach to Lean Six Sigma add to the practice of Appreciative Inquiry?

Let's start with the first question. The strength-based approach brings a huge benefit by introducing a different lens to the classic and commonly used thinking processes and tools of Lean Six Sigma. It expands the organization's ability to find, implement and, of course, to sustain solutions. How does it do so?

Focusing our analytical efforts (using the familiar Lean Six Sigma analytical tools) on identifying positive deviants of excellent perform-ance or understanding the root causes of success creates a positive shift in the conversation and a 'growth' mindset. The emphasis can shift from 'what went wrong and why' to 'where or when does this process/employee perform well/at its best and what enables it?' This expands our intellectual curiosity and allows more creativity from all involved. It creates a completely different level of engagement (imag-ine members of your organization being interviewed about their suc-cess and how that success can be repeated more consistently or built upon, as compared to being interviewed about their failures).

This approach does not ignore problems or defects. In order to overcome the defects, failures and wastes, it is far better to learn where we create perfection, success and value. Once operators and their managers understand what enables success, they are better placed to help recreate it, assisting sustainability and longer-term improvement. Understanding root causes of failure or wastes only gets us as far as *speculating* about what *might* solve the problem, and then trying that. Our speculations typically come from other areas of the operation or 'best practice' from elsewhere, instead of tapping into the internal tacit knowledge that undoubtedly exists in the system.

So then, how does the strength-based approach to Lean Six Sigma add to the general practice of Appreciative Inquiry, which has been developing and thriving around the world since the 1990s?

To many Appreciative Inquiry practitioners, the worlds of Lean Six Sigma and continuous improvement are foreign lands populated by negative, deficit-minded people. Appreciative Inquiry practitioners struggle to introduce and practise Appreciative Inquiry with these groups (by appreciating what they bring to the overall mix and by using their strengths) and it often seems (paraphrasing the title of a famous book) that 'Lean Six Sigma is from Mars and Appreciative Inquiry is from Venus'. I hope the following points will highlight, for those of us who come from the practice of Appreciative Inquiry, why we should build upon the immense wealth of knowledge and experience Lean Six Sigma practitioners offer:

1 Strength-based Lean Six Sigma helps introduce Appreciative Inquiry and strength-based thinking and practice while using language that most Lean Six Sigma change agents understand and can relate to. In addition, Lean Six Sigma uses approaches that most companies are comfortable with. Adding strength-focus to an existing framework that organizations are already comfortable with is far easier than introducing a new approach.

2 Lean Six Sigma has been around (in various forms and under different guises) for many years and has helped deliver change and improvements across the private and public sectors. Lean Six Sigma is a well-tested and documented practice for driving change and improvements. Appreciative Inquiry practitioners can learn a lot from the ways in which Lean Six Sigma practitioners test and monitor the impact of their practice.

3 Lean Six Sigma has a strong focus on analytics, metrics and quantitative data. Appreciative Inquiry practitioners can learn

from the analytical power Lean Six Sigma resources have and use it when analysis is needed to drive an Appreciative Inquiry initiative. I also find that classic Lean Six Sigma is more focused on the end results than strength-based change practitioners (who typically focus more on the journey of change and emergence). Lean Six Sigma can also offer ways to measure the effects of the change work (and potentially the impact of Appreciative Inquiry work).

4 Lean Six Sigma offers an important focus on the customers and what is valued by them. This is a good reminder for Appreciative Inquiry practitioners to include customers in our 'whole-system' approach to change.

5 Lean Six Sigma offers a structured and systematic approach to change that is comfortable for those inside organizations. The '5D' process (Define, Discover, Dream, Design, and Deliver) from Appreciative Inquiry, as robust as it is, can benefit from the systematic approach of Lean Six Sigma, in particular when it comes to designing and implementing solutions.

6 Strength-based Lean Six Sigma offers an opportunity, in great part untapped, for the expansion of strength-based change in organizations.

7 Finally Strength-based Lean Six Sigma offers the possibility of 'both/and' rather than 'either/or'. No longer do we have to choose one paradigm or the other – through Strength-based Lean Six Sigma we gain the benefits of both.

Summary

This chapter aimed to provide guidance on what forms a strength-based approach to Lean Six Sigma and why you should consider it. It also explored the benefits of combining the two ways of practice and thinking.

The next chapter will invite you to uncover and expand many assumptions that have guided us in our practice of Lean Six Sigma for many years.

The vision for a Strength-based Lean Six Sigma practice

08

Suppose every time we wish to drive organizational process improvement we take the strength-based approach instead of the classic approach to Lean Six Sigma... how different can our experience and the experience of the people we work with be? What outcomes can we reach? Would the outcome be better than what can be achieved through the classic approach? Will the route we take towards the changes be different? Easier perhaps? Would our people and customers respond differently? How would we know? What would be noticeably different?

In addition, what would happen if we consistently discovered or uncovered (sometimes even rediscovered) the 'positive core' of our organizational processes, the strengths the people who execute very complex processes have, or their aspirations?

Having practised Strength-based Lean Six Sigma for a few years, as well as collected evidence and stories from other practitioners, I am convinced that if, every time we look for ways to provide more value and greater quality for customers or improved flow in our processes, we use a strength-based approach rather than a deficit view, our outcomes will be better, new insights will emerge, the journey towards implementation and sustainability will be easier.

More than that, I now believe that we could get our processes to yield much more value than they could ever deliver before, getting ever closer to the most efficient way of using the resources invested in these processes and to providing unlimited value-add to customers. If we regularly ask how often a process performs well, seek what enables the better parts of our operations to perform at their best, or investigate cases of positive deviants, we shift to a completely new paradigm of thought and practice – one that generates energy, enthusiasm and creativity. A paradigm that is more resourceful, creative, full of energy and so far, from my experience, more successful...

Shifting to a new paradigm – key assumptions to reconsider

As I started the journey towards combining strength-based approach to change and Lean Six Sigma, I found myself reflecting on some deeper, more fundamental questions about the way I was taught about Lean Six Sigma and the way I had been practising it. For example:

1 Where did the story about, and endless focus on, 'waste removal' start?

2 Does a focus on removing defects offer the most efficient and effective way towards quality?

In fact, before I started this journey and even while I was developing my new thinking, almost all the conversations I had around Lean focused on wastes and waste removal – just look at any Lean-related discussion group or forum to see the keen interest in this topic.

My assumption is that practitioners, consultants and organizational leaders applied their own mental model and way of thinking to the stories they heard about Japanese practices. This way of thinking, which is particularly prevalent in the West, considers organizations and processes as being full of 'problems to be solved'.

I'm convinced that Lean Thinking in its origin was actually very aligned with the strength-based principles I described before. Where it may not have been, it still offered a good framework that could easily be reused positively by replacing the deficit-based content with new strength-based content.

This means that the typical practice of Lean Thinking and Six Sigma in the West is relying on some fundamental basic assumptions that dictate our direction of practice and may need to be reconsidered or perhaps replaced altogether. For example, Table 8.1 outlines the assumptions and an alternative strength-based viewpoint.

As a process improvement expert, I naturally accepted many of the underlying assumptions with the classic practice of Lean Six

TABLE 8.1 Underlying assumptions behind classic Lean Six Sigma vs a strength-based approach

Assumptions behind classic Lean Six Sigma	Alternative Strength-based assumptions
Organizations and processes are full of waste, defects or should be looked at as 'problems to be solved'.	Is it possible that organizations are full of interesting (well-hidden) surprises, accumulated knowledge and possibilities for endless learning and growth instead?
The current (or as-is) situation isn't as good as it can be. The best way forward is through reducing/shrinking our perceived problems (eg defect elimination or waste reduction).	The current situation is a great starting point for exploration. We can move forward faster and engage more people by growing our existing internal best practices and innovative practices (however few we believe we may have).
Process or organizational reality can be described objectively through collection and analysis of data which is then summarized and reported back. Being 'objective' means following scientific management – collecting facts, testing theories, drawing conclusions.	Is it possible that reality is constantly being created and redefined and is totally dependent on the conversations and viewpoints we and others have? People can construct the future they want by building strong relationships, developing powerful visions and by holding breakthrough conversations.
It is possible to separate 'fact finding'/data collection and analysis from decision making and 'actual change'.	Do many of the questions we ask immediately influence the direction of thinking and action thus resulting in an immediate change? Every question is in fact an intervention.

(continued)

TABLE 8.1 (Continued)

Assumptions behind classic Lean Six Sigma	Alternative Strength-based assumptions
Organizations or processes can be broken down to their components or building blocks in order to understand them better and be able to change them.	The beauty of our processes lies in their wholeness. Breaking them down to parts that are then changed or rearranged and then put back together doesn't actually create a 'better process' than before. Rather, it creates a completely new 'whole process' with its own reality of problems and possibilities.
Change is a result of careful and very detailed planning.	While careful planning has many merits, often change (and especially positive and engaging experiences of change) has a more emergent nature with unclear paths and with multiple leaders self-organizing.

Sigma. They were aligned with how I was brought up and with what I was taught at school, in university and throughout my career. Learning about Appreciative Inquiry was actually the first time I realized that what I took as given facts were actually only one way of thinking.

Similarly, for many people, Lean and Six Sigma are associated with 'eliminating waste', 'reducing costs', 'releasing head count' and 'minimizing the resources in the process' or reducing defects. However, all these terms are actually just good practices we have used for years because we take many assumptions for granted. I sometimes call this a deficit-based approach to Lean Six Sigma, although my preference is to simply call it 'classic Lean Six Sigma' (deficit isn't really an appreciative word is it?). I have a lot of respect for classic Lean Six Sigma – it has served me and the organizations I worked with very well over the years. Both perspectives are valid and useful in driving organizational improvement. Change strategies can benefit from both. In my view, with increasing experience over the past few years, a strength-approach is far more powerful.

A Strength-based Lean Six Sigma approach would adopt many alternative assumptions by asking different questions, by understanding that reality is always changing and emerging and can never be viewed as being static or 'objective'. More emphasis can be given to 'whole systems' and to the possibilities inherent in each situation.

Once we start asking a different type of question, we get different answers: new realities emerge, ideas sprout and energy levels and motivation increase. People start moving towards a more inspiring and exciting future, and they see themselves as essential contributors to the solution rather than being part of a problem to be solved.

Being Strength-based Lean Six Sigma (instead of thinking or doing)

Throughout my professional career journey, and in particular when I followed the Lean Six Sigma journey, I held the thought that for every process improvement situation I faced, there must be one (or a few) ways forward, and that if I were a good practitioner, I would be the 'expert' in finding the best tool to use in that situation. In other words, I should be the one who holds the torchlight that will illuminate the way forward towards the possible solutions. I believed that I should have as many 'tools' as possible in my toolbox – tools that would offer a useful approach to analysis and solution-finding. I had an insatiable hunger for new tools and always looked for 'best practices' in books, online or through conversations with other practitioners. The practice of Strength-based Lean Six Sigma taught me to shift my emphasis from total focus on 'thinking' to just 'being'. That means that observing, staying curious about the situation in front of me *as it is* and interested in others *as they are*, are actually far more important than searching for a solution through my own knowledge and collection of tools. Adopting a position of 'not knowing' rather than of 'an expert' is actually very liberating. It also helps better questions and observations to emerge. There is no need to worry about adopting this position thinking that you might not have the right tool or answer. If you hold a spirit of appreciation and inquiry, the right questions will come and the answers to these questions will raise incredible ideas and a fruitful dialogue! Some of these ideas may otherwise have stayed deeply buried.

Finally, it is essential to hold a belief in people's and organizations' strengths and endless capabilities or possibilities. If you hold to this belief, you will free yourself from a very transactional practice of Lean Six Sigma, where each problem has few potential solutions, to a much more rewarding experience of driving positive change and improvement.

Our key objectives – quality, flow and value

Product or service quality can be achieved in many ways. In the past, I certainly was able to raise the level of quality in the processes I worked on by identifying and resolving root causes of defects. Similarly, value-to-customer was raised by reducing waste, and flow by unblocking bottlenecks in the processes.

Of course, by now you can probably see that an equally good (and I argue much better) approach to quality is to spot and study existing perfection in products or services we supply to our customers (either internal or external). This still holds true even when these cases are relatively infrequent.

Flow of materials, people and information actually happens a lot more frequently than we realize when we focus on bottlenecks. Where can you spot free flow around the process you are working on? When did it flow well before? What enables/enabled it?

Many of the products and services provided by each organization and its people actually provide good value to customers. What makes it possible? How can you grow the best examples of such good value-add in front of you?

Remember, once you change the direction of your questions, you are very likely to come across different and relevant answers. Sometimes these answers will come from the most unexpected sources. Most people arrive at work with an aspiration to do a great job. Many of them indeed do a great job – sometimes their contribution is hidden very well. Now we can actually tap this great resource.

What about continuous learning and improvement?

Perhaps more importantly, in the longer term, we have the aspiration to drive the 'holy grail' of continuous improvement and learning (as compared to one-off changes). The common way to achieve this hope (to some degree) has been by holding a series of improvement workshops or projects in each area and carefully monitoring the outcomes (and often root cause analyses of what wasn't achieved). Do your clients or organization truly want to learn or just to 'do Lean on their processes/people'? Lean programmes are essentially about the organization learning to improve things rather than about 'experts' changing things on their behalf.

Of course, the strength-based approach to Lean Six Sigma offers a different style of continuous learning and improvement. The value of regularly identifying great practices (from the past and the present) as well as of identifying when a problem isn't actually happening is immense. Exploring (some may still want to call it analysing) what and who helps success, holding conversations around hoped-for visions for the future, and valuing the progress you make, are all great ways to continue the learning. Why not redefine continuous improvement away from solving one small problem at a time, to identifying something that works well and replicating or building on it, one step at a time?

Summary

In this chapter I wanted to expand as much as possible your views of what is possible with Strength-based Lean Six Sigma by shifting to a new paradigm of thinking about it, re-evaluating assumptions many of us take as given and highlighting the importance of 'being' and 'inquiring' over 'doing' or 'being an expert'. The next chapter will propose an additional exciting application of strength-based thinking to the area of performance metrics and scorecards.

What are you most curious about at this stage? Was there a particular assumption I talked about in this chapter that guided your practice or way of working for many years? What in your view can be the impact of taking the alternative assumption?

Strength-based metrics and performance review

09

Performance metrics are important to almost all organizations and over the past 20 years, have become widely known, used and tracked. Kaplan and Norton's balanced-scorecard approach has also been implemented with many organizations. Many of us spend our time at work completing tasks and projects that hopefully make a positive impact on one of the metrics our organization tracks and reviews regularly. Metrics enable everyone in the organization, regardless of their function, to understand how their work affects the organization's progress by providing a more visible link between individual or departmental performance and the goals of the organization.

Metrics and scorecards can be very powerful when they are used appropriately. The learning process required to create a useful scorecard and the data we collect and collate in charts help create meaning. The review conversations held around the scorecards generate insights and lead to better understanding of the organization's daily activities and outcomes. Strong and clear 'ownership' by members of the organization of each metric creates a greater sense of responsibility and a drive to act in the right direction. This improves commitment and energy towards the desired outcomes. However, this ownership needs to be seen in the context of the whole system, or else it can regress into disputed understanding of reality and required actions.

Applying a strength-based, appreciative approach to metrics can help maintain and sustain the spirit and energy created by the change initiatives we lead. Using metrics with an appreciative 'lens' together with strength-based questions can support growth and delivery of the desired outcomes, especially as various metrics are *already* used regularly to drive change and track progress. The application of strength-based principles and approach to metrics and scorecards transforms the way we refer to them, the conversations we hold around them and the impact they can make. As metrics often drive the priorities for improvement or change in the organization, there is a clear link between the approach we take to our scorecards and the approach we apply to improvement projects.

How to apply strength-based thinking to scorecards – a few pointers

There are several key thinking points to keep in mind when bringing a strength approach to organizational metrics.

1 Social construction

Unlike common belief, the value of data and measurements is not generated from reviewing the numbers or charts we produce but rather from the conversations we hold around them. As a practitioner analysing performance metrics, I was taught that being critical meant I was providing an objective point of view. In practice, it meant that I used to focus on the gaps, the weak performance points, the 'red-coloured' indicators and the data about customer complaints. This is not absolutely necessary! Being critical actually doesn't mean being objective. In fact, very rarely there is one, absolutely objective, view of a given reality. In most cases, there are many ways to observe and interpret reality. For example, De Bono's 'Six Hats' exercise (2000) is a useful example in showing us how reality can, at the same time, be viewed from several different angles. Most of my previously critical observations about the performance metrics were a result of my own habits. There is a lot we can learn from any chart and spreadsheet if we seek the strong points and the cases of stellar performance. Now, I choose to look at these data points and inquire about them not because I want to ignore the problems but rather because I am truly curious about the high points of success and believe they hold the most useful information.

Weak performance data points are also very useful. However, their usefulness is not so much in understanding what caused the problem. Rather, they are truly useful in asking ourselves and others what we wish to be different or what we want to change. This different focus generates different conversations within the organization leading to different images of the future. One image is of an organization constantly in struggle with its problems; the other an image of an organization that regularly defines how it wishes to be different and better!

2 What we focus on grows

What gets measured in an organization gets noticed and acted upon. This is not too dissimilar from the poetic and anticipatory principles that tell us that an organization moves in the direction we enquire about, and that actions are driven by strong images of the desired future. Targets set for metrics are certainly one of the ways to create an image of the desired future (or can be part of a bigger, more creative image of the future). Questions asked about high points of the past and present performance also aid teams and organizations in moving ahead.

3 The positive principle

Focus on the positive and what is wanted rather than the negative and what is not desired. Often, organizations measure indicators of problem areas they wish to see diminishing over time. For example, hospitals measure infection levels, manufacturers measure production defects and airlines measure the number of lost bags or minutes of delays. I used similar metrics before I knew about Appreciative Inquiry. However, we can make much more progress and gain more

FIGURE 9.1 The change journey when we focus on fixing what doesn't work

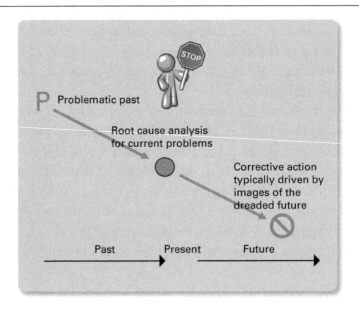

energy by measuring what we want to see more of, or what we want to increase over time. Members of the organization invest great effort in delivering improvements to our metrics. Questions are raised as well as answered and data are analysed to make meaning and find root causes. This is one way to learn from our current situation and improve it in the future. Imagine how different our conversations, actions and reality could look if hospitals measured cleanliness levels, manufacturers perfect production and airlines what helped deliver bags to their destination on time.

4 Simultaneity principle

Organizational change begins with our very first question. This is particularly important when we consider the review process of our scorecards, as often attention is paid to 'red' indicators while 'green' indicators are typically ignored or are mentioned casually. Instead, we can start our scorecard review by asking questions about what has become better since the last review. We can follow this by asking

FIGURE 9.2 The change journey when we start with what is working well

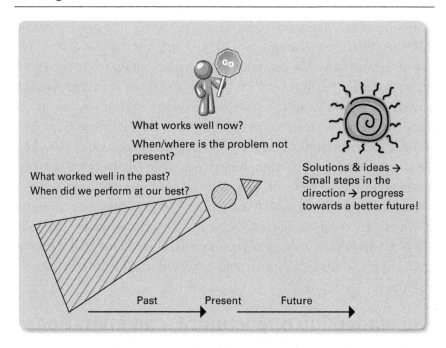

What works well now?

When/where is the problem not present?

What worked well in the past?
When did we perform at our best?

Solutions & ideas →
Small steps in the
direction → progress
towards a better future!

Past   Present   Future

how we can do more of it. This immediately transforms our attention and therefore actions towards an improved future.

5 Wholeness principle

Involving the whole system in defining and studying metrics as well as defining desired actions can promote true ownership and synchronized actions. In the past, I often facilitated small leadership teams (typically at the board level or the senior management of business units) through the definition stage and the review sessions. Other members of the organization were then told what metrics would be tracked, what the organization's targets for the year ahead would be and what strategies would be pursued. Imagine how much more powerful your scorecard could be if everyone in the organization truly understood what was being measured and why it was important.

6 *Organizations are living systems*

Reality is always changing within them and multiple views of the reality co-exist. Metrics we defined last year may not suit our needs this year. Often, by the time we obtain and analyse data, they are out of date anyway. We can take a step back, and remember that the main reason for having metrics in place is to encourage conversations leading to learning and continuous improvement. Rather than tying ourselves to set-in-stone targets and metrics, we can allow ourselves and our organizations to be less rigid about the scorecards. The key questions in defining meaningful metrics are: What do we need to measure now to achieve progress towards our current vision of the desired future? What would tell us, and others, that something is different? How would we and others know that we have achieved our goals and desired change? Or how would we know that we have made progress towards our dreams – what would be different then?

The leadership opportunity – an invitation to think and act differently

You may now wonder where to start in this journey of introducing an appreciative scorecard. What could be the first small step to take in order to move in this direction? How do you develop an interest in what works well in your organization and resist the temptation to focus on the negative?

If your organization is familiar with scorecards and the review process, introducing *different questions* offers a great opportunity for fostering *different conversations*. It helps what is already working well for the organization in terms of existing metrics and regular reviews while introducing a new angle. You have the options of:

1 Directing the attention towards the 'green' metrics: high points of performance and the periods when 'the problem is not present', understanding what 'gave life to' or enabled those situations. Being curious about strengths and high performance as well as 'positive deviants' can result in a fresh look at the existing data and may introduce new and useful insights for the future.

FIGURE 9.3 The benefit from focusing on positive deviants in performance

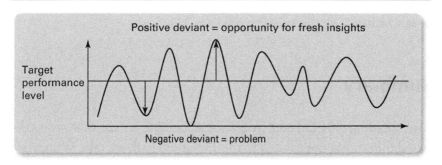

2 If your organization is drawn to analysing the lower points of performance, why not ask the following: 'Are there instances where this problem does not exist?' or 'Suppose we found a solution, how would it look? What would be different?'

If the organization is undertaking an appreciative approach to a particular change initiative or to its strategic planning process, make sure to include conversations to uncover the best, most generative, relevant metrics. When designing for its desired future, including generative metrics can lay the foundations for greater success as the organization takes particular actions towards its vision.

This way of thinking about metrics can also be useful when working with the SOAR (Strengths, Opportunities, Aspirations and Results) framework for strategic planning. When you hold conversations about the desired results, you can envision the best and most useful measurements that need to be introduced.

Some useful questions to include are: 'What do we want to see more of or to see increasing?', 'What would tell us that we are on track?' or 'What would be useful for us to measure in our desired future?' One of the benefits of this approach is the shared ownership by the whole system of the selected metrics.

It is important to keep in mind that some of these changes may take time to mature. Organizations familiar with deficit-orientated measurements may be surprised by the different focus proposed here. Other organizations may not be used to measurements and score-cards at all and will require training and time to adjust. Ultimately, the positive, strength-based focus for metrics and scorecards unleashes the natural curiosity, energy, desire to change and capacity to learn that is always present (though sometimes well hidden) within the organization.

Summary

After reading this chapter, you should be able to see that strength-based thinking is not limited to the analytical path we take in improving our operational and business processes. The thinking can have a greater scope and help us explore our organizational reality as portrayed by the metrics we monitor from a completely fresh direction, one that is more generative and enables growth and sustainability in the longer run.

The next chapter will offer further opportunities to apply strength-based thinking. The 'yellow brick road' of Strength-based Lean Six Sigma is expanding rapidly and is more inviting to travel along!

Approaches to Strength-based Lean Six Sigma

Both Appreciative Inquiry and Lean Six Sigma are systemic approaches to organizational change; both start with a view of the whole system. As we saw earlier, the desired outcomes from Lean Six Sigma programmes are positively framed. This alignment gives us multiple ways to combine the best of both worlds and apply the strength-based approach to Lean Six Sigma. The possible applications I have developed and present here are applicable to any of the following categories:

1 The whole organization.

2 A priority process.

3 A selected project.

4 The team involved with the project or those who are part of the process we target.

5 The tools used for analysis or for improvement.

In this chapter I will describe these categories and provide ideas for potential starting points. If you are familiar with Appreciative Inquiry terms, you can consider these to be 'micro provocative/possibility propositions'.

The whole organization

Most organizations have a strategic plan to guide their direction for the future. Developing a strategic plan using Appreciative Inquiry is a great way to create a meaningful plan and wider engagement with people across the whole system. Once we have the plan and know the priority areas of desired change, we can use either classic Lean Six Sigma or (better still) Strength-based Lean Six Sigma to implement some of the relevant changes. In this approach, we start with setting an overall inspiring direction for the whole organization and then use the strength of Lean Six Sigma/Strength-based Lean Six Sigma as a great implementation tool.

Another way to work at the whole-organization level is by developing *a shared vision of efficiency and quality* using Appreciative Inquiry, and similarly implementing the vision with Lean Six Sigma/ Strength-based Lean Six Sigma. Ideally, the vision of efficiency and quality is part of an overall strategic plan, but the topic can be approached independently. The Appreciative Inquiry process here would inquire into times when the organization, parts of it or its key processes performed very efficiently and at high levels of quality, finding out what enabled it at the time. It would also seek to learn from areas that are currently efficient and generate high-quality output. Finally, it would identify the wishes of members of the organization around quality and efficiency. We can also bring into this inquiry the users/customers of the organization's products and services. The vision of efficiency and quality in this case would be stronger and shared throughout the organization – a significantly better starting point than the more typical 'drop down' requirement for efficiency coming from the organization's leadership (or the government).

A separate way of integrating a strength-based approach into the whole organization by using strength-based metrics for the whole organization (ie metrics that track what we wish to see more of) is covered in detail in the previous chapter. This of course needs to be coupled with a strength-based performance review (looking at the high points, what enabled these achievements and what can be done to sustain or improve them even further).

Finally, for those organizations that have used classic Lean Six Sigma successfully over the years, we can use Appreciative Inquiry as a way of celebrating and learning from past successes and developing the 'next level': the next steps or next generation of the journey towards efficiency and quality using an Appreciative Inquiry process.

A priority process

If you have prioritized specific organizational processes for improvements, there are several ways to integrate Strength-based Lean Six Sigma thinking with improvement efforts.

You can start by creating a dream or vision of the 'best that can be' for the selected process using Appreciative Inquiry thinking. Once you have the vision to guide you and the improvement team, it is easier to follow the Lean or Strength-based Lean route for implementation. Selecting the right tool from your tool box should be easier in this case: you will know which direction for improvement the people involved with the process would like to take.

When looking at a process, it can be very useful to find out what makes the people involved in the process 'flow' (some prefer 'be in the zone'). Do we know which parts of the process employees feel most passionate about? What do they love getting involved with? Uncovering these insights can be very useful.

Often I choose to integrate strength-based questions or an interview process focused on the process I was tasked with improving. An example for such an interview can be found on page 118.

Another way is to facilitate a strength-based Kaizen event/blitz or a 'workout' session instead of a classic Kaizen or workout workshop. One key element of the process is integrating Appreciative Inquiry questions when studying the 'as is' situation. You can also integrate a strength-based process-mapping or value-stream map (ie focusing the attention and the conversation on the better parts of the process, identifying what enabled them and how to do more of the same or expand these great practices elsewhere). Finally, a good tool to use, particularly when asking participants to 'go see' is 'the Seven Signs of Value'. This tool is explained in the next chapter.

Appreciative Interview for a process

This interview guide can be used as part of a Kaizen event or independently with a process operator. The questions included in this guide are flexible and can be adjusted as required for your situation:

1 Think of a time when this process was at its best. It can be a specific experience you had when either you, or this process, were delivering great results or when you were most proud about this work. The experience can be recent or from the past:

 – What was happening then?

 – What did you do that helped the situation?

 – Who helped/supported the good outcome?

 – What else made it possible?

 – What can you learn from this story that is useful *now*?

2 What is working well today? Where and when does this process deliver value to customers?

3 What do you specifically value about the current setup or design of the process and activities taking place?

4 Where in this process are parts and information flowing well? Where are tasks completed easily and consistently at high quality?

5 How can we provide more value or better quality to the customers of this process?

6 If you had the ability to improve this process as you wish, what would you improve first? How would the process look then?

In this way, we are using the best knowledge there is – internal knowledge, rather than bringing external best practices that may or may not be relevant and are more likely to generate resistance.

A project

When we already have a project that was selected and scoped out of multiple opportunities for improvement, we can still bring the strength-based approach. The first option is to explore the possibilities to reframe the topic for improvement. Appreciative Inquiry emphasizes the importance of selecting positive and inspiring topics for inquiries (improvement projects are essentially inquiry processes). Solution Focus also emphasizes the importance of clearly identifying what we wish to move towards. Repeatedly asking questions such as 'What would be better?' or 'What else would you like to see when we complete this project successfully?' yield a better, more inspiring goal to help us through the more challenging parts of our project. For example, in the Internet Service Provider case story described in Chapter 4 we demonstrated how a project goal changed from 'reducing customer complaints' to 'having no complaints' (first iteration) and then to a final topic of 'having perfect connections'. This is certainly a more inspiring topic. It also helped generate much more enthusiasm than the previous two.

Once we start our project, we can alter the focus of the inquiry/analysis. In this case, we could look at the positive outcomes of the process we have targeted and try to understand them, rather than the defects. In other words, seek to understand why 80 per cent works well versus the 20 per cent that is defective.

Another great source of insights can come from identifying, learning from and expanding examples of positive deviances (cases of stellar performance). However rare they may be, there are normally positive deviants to be found. Their existence can lead us into a very productive line of inquiry and generate useful insights for improvement.

Finally, I often use an Appreciative Inquiry (e)valuation process to learn from the progress achieved through a Lean Six Sigma project. For example, refer to the interview on the next page.

The main reason to use a strength-based valuation process is that, regardless of the outcomes of the project, we can still learn from the process we followed; in cases where the project was successful, we can help the outcomes become more sustainable by inquiring into the success. If, however, the project is regarded as a less-than-successful experience, using the valuation approach would ensure that at least the project retains some useful learning and commitment towards future projects.

This is a sample appreciative interview guide that can be used to evaluate the progress made through a Kaizen event, a project or another concentrated improvement effort. The interview can start with a positive framing. I use something like the following:

As you can remember, a few weeks ago, we conducted a Kaizen event (or a project) that focused on improving [complete the name of the process or area accordingly].

Looking at all the great things we've been able to accomplish since we began this improvement journey, during the event and afterwards:

1 Tell me of a specific experience or time when you noticed an improvement in the process:

   – What was happening?

   – What were you doing?

   – What were others doing?

   – What made it better from your perspective?

2 On a scale of 1–10, how close are we to the 'future perfect' (equals a rating of 10)? How did we make all this great progress?

3 What do you value the most in this improvement experience? How has this experience benefited you personally? Your team? The organization? Our customers?

4 What is the best way to sustain the progress we've made?

5 What three wishes do you have that would enable further improvement to this process or to other processes?

The project or process team

Most improvement initiatives require teams to be set up for the purpose of completing a project or even for the short term of a Kaizen event. We can start the path of improvement with a stronger and better performing team by using an Appreciative Inquiry approach to team development. We can also use any of the strength-finding assessment tools available for individuals and teams to discover and share existing strengths in the improvement team, or within the team operating the process we are focusing on.

Along our journey towards improvement, there are many moments when we stop to reflect about where we are as a team, what we have achieved so far and what we haven't yet achieved. It's a great way to recalibrate our efforts. We can use the Appreciative Inquiry or Solution Focus processes to aid these reflection points and to inject fresh energy (often, energy levels are lowest in the middle of improvement projects). We can inquire into our progress and learning so far, find out what we value about the work of the team, identify the strengths we have seen in our work together, and generate new wishes to move forward towards completion.

Finally, it helps if the leadership at the shop-floor level integrates a different set of questions when interacting with shop-floor staff, question that focus on strengths (human level) and best levels of performance (operational level).

The tools we use

As described in our tools section (see Chapter 11), many classic Lean Six Sigma tools can be completely changed by integrating the strength focus. This means that we highlight what we want to see more of, as well as asking strength-orientated (instead of deficit-focused) questions. For example, I have created and used 'the Seven Signs of Value' (based, of course, on the 'Seven Wastes') as well as 'Wishbone' analysis ('Fishbone'/*Ishikawa* diagram, page 128). The tools section of this book covers a few examples; more tools are available online on our website (www.almond-insight.com/category/blog).

Another way forward is by using the excellent Solution Focus tool called 'small steps' to help with implementing big ideas when we reach the implementation phase.

Essentially, any process or tool that requires data collection, sourcing opinions, rating/prioritizing possibilities and options, or reflection/review, can be used with a strength focus. Using Appreciative Inquiry or Solution Focus questions can help us achieve acceptance and engagement.

Getting started

Having read this chapter, what are you curious about? Where is the waste or where is the potential value in your organizational processes (or perhaps both)? I hope that by offering you the ways discussed above to integrate strength-thinking with Lean Six Sigma, I piqued your curiosity and interest in experimenting.

Feel free to start at the level that is relevant to your situation. For example, if you are just embarking on a Lean journey, you could benefit from starting with level one (the whole organization). If your organization has already prioritized processes for improvement or set up improvement project areas, you can take the process/project route. The team level can also be useful to apply.

Finally, if you already have Lean Six Sigma projects in progress, you may wish to select and use a few strength-based tools to aid your analysis, bring new insights and support the improvement effort. Of course, your choice also needs to reflect specific issues, applications and existing knowledge as well as your experience with strength-based approaches and the comfort level of the person applying them. The key message is: taking any of these approaches can help your quality and efficiency objectives.

Summary

In this chapter I have shown you the breadth of possible applications of a strength-based approach to Lean Six Sigma. You can apply the thinking at multiple levels and gain many new insights as well as enhanced engagement from your improvement project teams.

This chapter also marks the conclusion of the third part of this book – the 'Dream' segment – in which we have explored and uncovered the best of 'what can be'. I did so by describing the characteristics underlining Strength-based Lean Six Sigma practice; by introducing alternative, more generative assumptions to guide you, through offering new Lean Six Sigma processes; and by suggesting possible applications of the strength-based approach to performance metrics. Finally, I also highlighted many 'provocative propositions' for applying strength-based thinking.

Before you move to the next part of the book, which will focus on more concrete steps towards implementing what we have covered in this part (for example, new strength-based tools and a complete design for a strength-based Kaizen), I invite you to reflect on the following questions:

1 In what way is the dream of Strength-based Lean Six Sigma challenging what I already know or inviting me to grow?

2 How can it help my organization or my clients?

3 What do I need to change or add to my practice?

4 What will it enable me to do or achieve? What is its promise?

5 In what ways can Strength-based Lean Six Sigma be useful or add value to everything I already do and know?

6 Where should I start? What could be my first step?

PART FOUR
Design

The purpose of the 'Design' stage of an inquiry is to create bridges between the inspiring possibilities we uncover in the 'Dream' part and what will eventually be implemented. We focus on identifying the design elements that are essential to bring the dream to reality.

Chapter 11 begins the Design section by suggesting concrete, step-by-step ways to use Lean Six Sigma tools from a strength-based approach. We already touched on the possibility of doing so in the last chapter; now I'll show you how to do it.

The next chapter offers ways to integrate strength-based thinking with Lean and Six Sigma's most common frameworks as well as how to integrate Lean and Six Sigma with Appreciative Inquiry's 5D framework.

Finally, Chapter 13 provides a detailed design for a strength-based Kaizen. Many of us have either delivered or experienced the benefits of the Kaizen approach. Now it is time to freshen up the approach with strength-based elements!

The Strength-based Lean Six Sigma Tools

"The way people think is far more important than the tools they use."
Dennis Pawley, Former Chrysler Executive

This chapter explores some of the common Lean Six Sigma tools that have been transformed by applying strength-based thinking to them. The easiest way to try Strength-based Lean Six Sigma is by bringing a new twist to a well-known and familiar tool with which you as a practitioner or the people you work with feel comfortable. For example, SOAR (Strength, Opportunities, Aspirations, Results), which was created by Jackie Stavros, is a strength-based version of the well-known SWOT analysis, transforming it into a more useful and versatile tool.

In this chapter I offer the following tools:

1 'Wishbone' analysis – a strength-based version of the 'fishbone' analysis tool.

2 'Value walk' – a strength-based version of the 'waste walk'.

3 Strength-based process (or value-stream) mapping.

4 A strength-based Gemba/Genbutsu ('go see') process.

5 Strength-based 'Five-Why's'.

6 A strength-based A3 Template.

There are more examples available on our blog (www.almond-insight.com/SBLSS/blog/) and LinkedIn group (called 'Strength Based Lean Six Sigma').

Typically, integrating Appreciative Inquiry principles into most Lean Six Sigma tools changes their purpose and often makes them more powerful in generating useful insights for improvement. For each of the tools above, I will offer a suggested way to apply it, its new purpose and additional insights I have gained by using it. Readers are welcome to try out these Strength-based Lean Six Sigma tools, as well as invent their own tools.

Wishbone analysis/success cause analysis

The 'fishbone analysis' is commonly used to identify and map cause-and-effect relationships; we can apply the same analytical process to identify contributors/root causes to either:

1 an identified successful outcome we would like to understand better; or

2 a possibility, wish, hope or vision statement.

What does it look like?

FIGURE 11.1 Two versions of strength-based wishbone diagrams

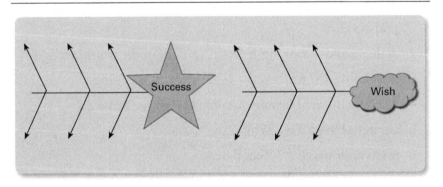

Suggested process and questions

To perform a 'success cause analysis', start from the outcome that has already happened and link it to the key enablers (main 'bones'.) Continue the analysis to identify what made each one of these key enablers possible (small 'bones'.) This process can point you in the direction of *design requirements* that are essential to repeat the success. For example, you can use the following questions:

- Who or what contributed to this success?
- What enabled this to happen?
- What made it possible?
- What else?

These questions are particularly useful as you carry out the process.

For a wishbone analysis, pick possibility statements or a wish from your Appreciative Inquiry process. The possibility statements you are starting with should preferably be more detailed ('micro level' statements) than the overall dream statement of a typical Appreciative Inquiry ('macro level'). Start by linking it to all the key areas you will need to work on to bring life to this wish. Continue this process by linking these key areas all the way to actual actions.

Purpose

Using this tool offers us a shared learning, growth and change experience by appreciating recent cases of success. It can also be used as a Design tool to help us identify what needs to be worked on to deliver our dreams/possibility statements.

Additional insights

You can use the same headline categories you may be familiar with from using fishbone analysis in the past. I sometimes use the following categories: equipment, process, people, materials, environment, and management. Other options include the 4 Ms (machine, method, material, and manpower) with additional optional Ms (as required in the situation) such as: mother nature, measurement, maintenance, money and management. There are also the 6Ps: product/service, price/cost, place, promotion, people and process. Remember also that you can invite the participants to create categories relevant to their own case (thus appreciating their knowledge and ability to create categories meaningful to them.)

Ultimately, the change that will be implemented is not necessarily a direct outcome of this activity. Not everything can be linked in a 'cause-and-effect' connection. However, this tool and the conversations it generates help participants articulate, dream and design together what needs to be implemented for the dream to come true (a great help when a group is trying to make sense and progress with their wishes).

The 'value walk' and the 'seven signs of value'

One of the most common Lean Thinking tools is the 'waste walk'. Here, participants in an improvement workshop or a Kaizen event are asked to identify all sources of waste as they follow a selected process. Waste walks typically follow the process as it is performed on the ground or, as an alternative, using a process map. Waste is broadly defined as any activity that adds costs or complexity without adding value to the products or services that the company offers its customers. The search for waste in processes follows the seven types of waste as defined in Lean Thinking: defects, overproduction, unnecessary transportation, waiting, inventory, unnecessary motion, and over-processing. This waste-elimination effort typically alleviates the pain the organization feels in the shorter term. However, the waste never seems to go away. In many cases, new forms of waste are generated or discovered!

I have already explained how the use of positive language and compelling images can be a powerful engine for change. It is also well documented that our brains are far better at processing and responding to a positive affirmation (for example: 'I'm going to hit the ball right on target') than they are at processing and responding to a negative affirmation ('I should not hit the trees at the back.') This knowledge is widely used in the area of performance coaching (and especially in sports coaching).

If negative affirmations are proven to reduce the chances of achieving superior performance in sports, it is also possible that they reduce our chance of success in our process-improvement initiative. Instead of teaching people how to identify everything we *do not want* to have in our processes, we could point out to them the signs of good processes or, better still, give them the tools to appreciate what is working in their own environment.

If we apply this thinking to the 'waste walk' tool, we can completely transform it to the 'value walk' by looking for and identifying where value is created – which is what we *want to see more of*. This would mean that we would be looking for the following seven signs of value:

1 **Perfection.** Parts of the process where perfect outcomes are generated regularly.

2 **Exact production.** Where operators produce exactly what is needed for the next step.

3 **Shortest distance travelled.** Where information, parts or people either stay where they are needed or travel the shortest distance possible.

4 **Just in time.** Where parts or information are provided only when needed.

5 **The right quantity.** When we get the right amount of parts or information to complete the task.

6 **Easy to reach and pass on.** When parts, tools or information are kept where we need them.

7 **Simplicity.** When process steps are completed in the simplest way possible.

Always remember that value is defined from the point of view of the customer of a given process or process step.

FIGURE 11.2 The seven signs of value generate more value to customer

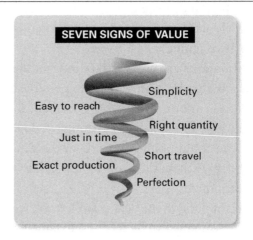

What does it look like?

The examples of value should come from the actual process being improved so that the improvement team will gain the confidence about that particular process. By learning from current good practices and expanding them, we ensure a smoother transition from the 'as is' situation to the desired 'to be' state.

A new purpose for the tool

By identifying where value is created in a given process and inquiring into what enables it, we focus the attention on what we want to see *more of*. The immediate result is a learning process and potential ideas for opportunities to expand the value creation, thus providing greater value to our customers. Positive side effects include higher motivation and greater focus on value creation elsewhere.

Suggested process and questions

There are many ways to use the tool. For example, a value walk can be easily included as part of a process-improvement workshop ('Kaizen event'). I normally ask participants or members of an organization to identify examples of each value and inquire into its root causes (ie What enables it?). I also ask 'How can we expand this to other parts of the process?' or 'Where else can we apply this?' There are many appreciative and strength-based variations of questions that come handy when using this tool.

Finally, the seven signs of value are also useful as a reference when pursuing continuous improvement across an organization.

Process/value-stream mapping

There are many versions of process or value-stream maps. When mapping a process, the emphasis is always on mapping it *as it is* rather than how it should or could be. However, nothing prevents us from mapping the process as it is *when it is working well*!

Suggested process and questions

The following is a suggested strength-based version of a mapping process that I use in improvement workshops.

I start by mapping the process steps in as much detail as possible. Mapping the steps can start from the end point or from the very beginning of the process. Under each process step, using a sticky note with a different colour, I ask participants to identify the current cycle time. These first steps are identical in both classic and strength-based approaches. However, the next few steps are very different.

Next, I ask the participants (again, using a different-coloured sticky note) to write, for each process step, what is the best cycle time they (or someone else) has been able to achieve for that step.

I then follow by asking what inputs are required to complete each step successfully and what the current success rate is.

Finally, for each step, we identify the strengths and opportunities for improvement. Opportunities for improvement are framed with the following question: 'What could make this step even more successful?'

At this stage additional, general ideas for improvement (ie ideas that apply to the whole process rather than a specific step) also surface – I ask participants to capture them as well.

What does it look like?

The end result of the map may look like this:

FIGURE 11.3 Strength-based value stream map

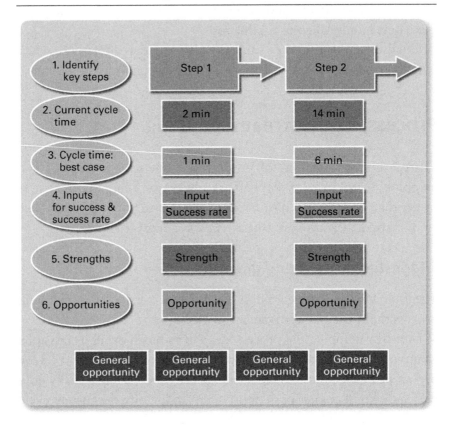

A new purpose for the tool

Process mapping has always been one of my favourite improvement tools. It gives everyone a common language and a shared understanding of how a given process is performed and what can be done to improve it. The strength-based version I propose and use has the same benefit. At the same time, it instils confidence in those who complete it that improvement is indeed possible, as well as within reach, as light is shed specifically on the better parts of the process. In addition, we do not ignore the problems or challenges in the process but frame them as an opportunity for further improvement or a wish for a better future. The different framing encourages people to more naturally (and often more creatively) come up with and adopt the required changes.

Additional insights

Whenever possible, I apply the principle of Wholeness by ensuring the whole system involved with the process is part of the mapping and analysis process. This ensures we get more (and real) insights as well as greater engagement with the change process.

Gemba/Genbutsu ('go see')

The practice of Gemba (or Genba) or Genbutsu is expressed in English as 'go see' or 'go to the real place'. The real place is where the product is being made, where a service is being provided, or where interactions with customers are happening. Lean practitioners emphasize the importance of 'go see' for two reasons:

1 The role of management is to spend as much time as possible in the Gemba to get a better understanding of what is really happening.

2 When running process-improvement workshops, as much as possible, run them in the Gemba.

A very powerful strength-based approach to the Gemba is possible by integrating it with the SOAR process, which adds an excellent thinking framework. It is possible to do it either through self-reflection (as is often favoured by the original Lean practitioners in Japan who practice the Gemba) or as a framework for a dialogue with an operator on the shop floor. Some useful questions to include in your Gemba process in order to get the 'real place' SOARing are:

Strengths

- What strengths, assets, creativity and qualities can be observed in this workstation, with this operator or process?
- What is currently working well? What can be built upon?
- What are you proud of?
- What was the peak performance level observed or recorded? What enabled it?

- What unique skills are evident? What useful ideas can I gain here?
- How was a recent issue/problem/challenge overcome?
- What is going well and should be kept as is?

Opportunities

- What ideas do you already have to make this workstation, operator or process even better?
- What advice do you get from others?
- Suppose a customer (or even a competitor) were to visit or observe this area, what would they have suggested?
- In your opinion, what else needs to happen here to make it better?
- If this operator, workstation or process was operating in the best, most efficient and effective way, what would be different? What else?
- What can be expanded or developed here?

Aspirations

- What are your best hopes for this workstation, process and operator?
- How do you wish this process, workstation or operator to improve or be different in three years?
- If you had three wishes for this process, workstation or operator what would they be?
- What does the operator at this workstation wish to see changed?

Results

- What would indicate to us that this operator, workstation or process has improved? What else?
- What results do we wish to see here?
- When this process has reached a better stage, what will be noticeably better?
- Suppose this process somehow operated at its best possible state, what results would it produce? How?

In fact, you can even add an additional line of inquiry by adding another 'R' to SOAR: this additional R represents the 'Resources' available to you in order to move forward towards some of the aspirations and desired results.

Note that although I propose the Appreciative Inquiry SOAR approach, the actual questions I use come from both Appreciative Inquiry and Solution Focus.

Strength-based five-why's

The five-why's is one of the easiest and most commonly used problem-solving tools. In the classic application of the tool, when a problem occurs, we are prompted to ask 'why did it happen?' When an answer is given, we follow it by asking 'why' again, this time to ask why the answer we were given occurred, and so on. The rule of thumb many practitioners follow is that after asking 'why' five times, we will get to the bottom of the problem, and we should be able to point to its true root cause.

The strength-based approach to using this tool is actually very simple: in fact, no change is required. We still ask 'why' five times. However, the key is in the choice of topic to focus on. To solve a problem, we first reframe the question to a situation where the problem didn't exist. We then identify what *did* exist instead. Once we know what existed in place of the problem, we can ask 'Why did it exist?' and continue the line of inquiry as usual. In fact, this tool and the thinking process it follows resembles the 'Small Steps' tool from the Solution Focus toolbox.

A3 template

A3 templates are commonly used as a problem-solving tool. The steps followed in the template are very simple and essentially follow the PDCA (plan-do-check-act) cycle. The power of the template lies in its relative simplicity and the ability to include all the required information for understanding the problem and the plan of action on one (albeit slightly larger than standard) piece of paper.

A3 template - an example

Title: *What are you talking about?*

Starting Situation:

What would you like to work/are you working on? What is the situation? Who wants this situation to be different? Who would benefit from it? How? Provide facts, metrics & costs.

What works already?

Identify any 'counters' and 'resources': what skills, experience and know-how is available? In what situation does the problem not occur or is it less intense?

Vision (Preferred Future):

Suppose this problem didn't exist, how would this situation, process or area look? What would be different?

Scale:

On a scale from 1–10 rate the current situation and where you want to be in comparison to the preferred future.

Current situation	Where you want to be	Preferred future
		10

Action plan:

What needs to be done to move forward?

What	Who	When	First smallest, concrete step

Results:

What results has the action plan had on the initial metrics and starting situation?

Learning:

What have you noticed when solving this problem? What surprised and delighted you?

Next steps?

What next steps are now possible that you didn't expect before solving the situation?

As you can see on the previous two pages, this problem-solving template can be used from a strength-based approach. This A3 template was proposed by Nicolas Stampf, a friend and a key 'thinking partner' in my Strength-based Lean Six Sigma learning journey.

Notice how nicely Solution Focus tools and questions fit into the flow of inquiry in this template. In addition, this process opens the door for further learning and improvement rather than completing the process when the problem is solved, enabling *continuous improvement*!

Summary

By now, I am sure you can see that there are many ways to integrate strength-based thinking while practising Lean Six Sigma and bring more life to it. This is especially true for the improvement tools we use. Strength-based Lean Six Sigma is essentially socially constructed and ever-changing, thus allowing each application to become unique.

In this chapter I chose to focus on six commonly used tools. However, many other tools can be made 'strength-based' by:

- changing the focus point from failures, weaknesses, defects and wastes to high points of performance, perfection and success;

- changing the questions used to gather and analyse information;

- making different choices around what we notice (good practices and internal knowledge, examples when the problem does not occur).

For example, even an FMEA (Failure Modes Effects Analysis) can become an SMEA (Success Mode Effects Analysis.) Let's spend our time and energy studying success and finding ways to amplify it!

I invite each one of you to apply your creativity and come up with your own tools, and to share your innovations with us so that we can learn as well. Developing additional tools will be even more useful as we move to the next two chapters, which propose strength-based approaches to the DMAIC or PDCA improvement cycles as well as a potential design for a Kaizen event. As you probably know, Kaizen events may require different tools each time we hold them, depending on the desired outcomes.

The Strength-based Lean Six Sigma process – classic frameworks with a fresh twist

12

There are many ways to integrate generative questions, Appreciative Inquiry processes, Solution Focus thinking and dialogue-based techniques within the common Lean Thinking and Six Sigma frameworks. Adding a strength-based approach to the well-known DMAIC and PDCA cycles can completely change the direction of inquiry and add more energy and creativity.

In this chapter I focus on two well-known Lean and Six Sigma thinking processes – PDCA and DMAIC – as well as the Appreciative Inquiry 5D cycle, and highlight how to integrate strength-based thinking with the first two or Lean Six Sigma with the latter. There are many other widely used frameworks but the ones I mentioned above are possibly the most common and my suggestions for them can easily be adapted to other frameworks.

FIGURE 12.1 The PDCA cycle step-by-step

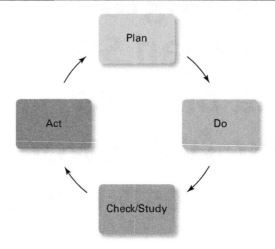

PDCA/PDSA

'Plan Do Check Act' (PDCA) is a well-known cycle for problem solving and continuous improvement. It was originally introduced by Deming as a systematic approach to improvement. Sometimes it is also referred to as PDSA (Plan Do Study Act). In its original application, it is an iterative process of expansion, learning and improvement where each cycle adds more insights and knowledge that become useful in further improving the product or service at hand.

The question is, can we combine the PDCA cycle with the questions we ask when using strength-focused methods? In my view they can go very well together. All strength-based approaches to change are essentially spiral rather than linear, which is also true to the PDCA approach.

The strength-based approach to PDCA creates a cycle of 'generative continuous improvement'. It studies 'what is best' in order to help us identify and move toward 'what is next'. This can be done in all aspects – the process, enabling relationships, productivity, and costs.

In order to identify how to integrate strength-based thinking with the PDCA process, I will start by identifying the purpose of each step and then provide ideas on how to bring in the new thinking in order to support each step's purpose:

1 *Plan*

The purpose of this step is to identify the actions to take and processes to implement in order to achieve a desired outcome or result. If we start with a specific desired outcome or result, how can we follow with Appreciative Inquiry? First, the desired outcome can be phrased as an affirmative topic for inquiry. You can then follow with the first three steps of the 4D cycle, which are Discover, Dream and Design. Start by discovering the 'best of what is'. In other words, when have you experienced the highest level of performance? When have you performed at a level that is closest to the desired level or even at levels exceeding the desired level? What enabled it in the past? What strengths are existing in the area we are focusing on that could help us move closer to the desired outcomes? And so on. We then 'Dream' of the 'best that could be' based on all this rich information. The dream helps in expanding our thinking even beyond the goal we started with. We follow the dream phase with a 'Design' phase, which is where we plan how to reach the dream by identifying the key design elements we wish to develop and implement. The Design phase is actually not too dissimilar to the one taken in the original PDCA; however, notice how the expansive nature of the discovery and dream phases can sometimes take us further than the classic 'Plan' phase would. Another approach to the Plan step is by using some of the Solution Focus tools. For example: the desired outcome can be identified through the 'Platform' and 'Future Perfect' tools while the 'Scaling', 'Small Actions' and 'Counters' could be an excellent source for ideas on what to try in order to move in the direction of the desired outcomes.

2 *Do*

In this step we implement the plan we defined in Step 1. As a result of implementing the plan the reality has changed. We complete this step by collecting data that reflects the current situation. This step is very similar to the 'Deliver' step of Appreciative Inquiry. Alternatively, another great way forward is to take the first few 'small steps' that emerged from the 'Plan' stage. It is important to notice the impact of these changes and to do so from a strength-based point of view. This means that you should notice what has changed for the better as a result of what you did. Any data that indicates a positive movement is useful. This also includes narrative/qualitative data, which is often ignored or doesn't get the attention it deserves compared with numeric data.

3 Check/Study

In this step we check that the outcomes of the changes we implemented at the 'Do' step have delivered the results we wished for, or have at least brought us closer. By analysing the data, finding patterns and comparing the results we delivered with the results we planned for, we hope to obtain the 'full picture' and understand what we need to do next in order to get even closer to the hoped-for results. The objective of learning from the changes we implemented can be achieved by an Appreciative Inquiry (e)valuation of the experiment we conducted earlier. We can use questions such as: 'What has been the best experience as a result of the change we implemented?'; 'What were the greatest results?'; 'What is particularly valuable in the new design we implemented?'; 'What is appreciated by the customers and by everyone involved with this process?'; 'What have we learned in this cycle of change that can be useful elsewhere?'; and finally, 'What three things could help us make it even better next time?' The Solution Focus approach to check/study may involve the use of the 'Counters' and 'Affirm' tools by identifying: 'What is better now?'; 'What else is better?'; and, 'How were we able to achieve this?' Notice the nice addition of 'What else is better?' from Solution Focus – often we can find several aspects that are better.

4 Act

In this step we follow through the conclusions that emerged from the last step. Essentially we either adjust the original plan or identify further new steps that can be taken to move forward from where we are now.

How to follow up on the conclusions from the 'Check/Study' step? From an Appreciative Inquiry point of view, you can essentially define a new affirmative topic of inquiry based on what emerged from the last step and start a new cycle of discovery and expansion using the 5Ds process. Another alternative is to identify the best outcomes we now have achieved and design ways to expand them to increase the level of success. If you wish to take the Solution Focus approach, you can identify where you are now on the original 'Scale' compared to the original 'Future Perfect'; although it would probably be a better approach to identify a fresh 'Future Perfect' – you may find that you have a better and bigger view of what the 'Future Perfect' is, now that you have been through the full cycle at least once.

The 'DCCA cycle' – could this be the new PDCA?

In a recent workshop, I asked participants to imagine new strength-based possibilities for their way of using the PDCA cycle. One of the ideas that emerged was very interesting. The suggestion was to create a cycle titled DCCA, which would consist of:

1. **Dream/Design.** In this phase we envision what is wanted and identify potential ways to move forward.

2. **Create/Deliver.** We follow the first step by innovating and creating, thus delivering an actual positive change.

3. **Celebrate.** After the creative step, we identify the improvements we made, celebrate the achievements and mark all the strengths and skills we found during the delivery.

4. **Accelerate.** Having celebrated, we identify ways to accelerate and expand the positive impact as well as further develop the existing strengths.

Naturally, all of the above steps can be infused with strength-based questions and thinking processes similar to the ones I proposed above for PDCA.

Notice how going through the PDCA/PDSA cycle with an Appreciative Inquiry or a Solution Focus approach gives you direct information on ideas about what works, what is wanted and what would take the situation forward. In comparison, the classic approach to PDCA/PDSA is more speculative: it indicates 'what is not working' or 'what is not wanted' as well as 'what causes the process to fail or underperform' – these are of course useful insights although they do not indicate what could work instead.

In addition, we are redefining the meaning of continuous improvement. By taking a strength-based approach, we switch from solving one small problem at a time to taking one small working idea and replicating it, one at a time. In addition to replicating, the actual inquiry into 'what works well' helps expand the possibilities...

DMAIC

FIGURE 12.2 The DMAIC process-improvement steps

The DMAIC improvement cycle is at the heart of the Six Sigma methodology. It is also regularly used for Lean Thinking process-improvement initiatives. Although the classic version of this process is very deficit-based and focuses our attention on the specific problem we wish to solve along with its root causes, it is possible to follow the DMAIC cycle using a strength-based approach. Below, I propose one way to do so with the intention that you tailor it to your needs, situation and best understanding of strength-based tools, approaches and principles.

Define

The purpose of this step is to define a specific problem that we wish to solve, set the goals for the project, identify what is important to the customer of the process (by collecting VoC – Voice-of-Customer), agree the scope of the project, expected timelines, and the business case for change (ie the expected benefit to the business). All this important information is normally collected in a document called the 'project charter'.

A strength-based approach would start by defining the desired outcome we wish to move towards (rather than the more commonly used 'problem statement' we wish to address and move away from). This can be done through strength-based interviewing (using an Appreciative Inquiry discovery interview or Solution Focus 'Platform' and 'Future Perfect' questions). The target audience for these interviews would be the project sponsor, the process owner (if one exists) and employees involved in the process. The interviews would help us reveal the positive core of those involved and of the process itself, uncovering people's motivation for change and helping generate engagement with future changes.

Next we collect the voice of the customer. There are many ways to complete this important step. If you are starting with reactive and existing data (for example from customer complaints or past surveys) make sure you note what the customer specifically wanted rather than what was not wanted. You may need to reframe the data at hand or your understanding of it to get the right focus. Remember, knowing what is not wanted doesn't necessarily indicate what is! If you decide to proactively collect new data, you can easily use simple questions such as: 'What has been your best experience using our products or services or of interacting with us as your supplier?', 'Suppose we were able to provide you with the ideal product/service, in what ways would it be different?' and 'If you were able to change three things that would make your experience even better, what would they be?'

Depending on the time available with customers, you can add additional questions as required. The Six Sigma belt who is leading the project together with the project team (which ideally is representative of the process, its suppliers and its customers) can then make sense of the data collected through the interviews and set the project goals. Make sure that throughout the project charter, a strength-based, generative and affirmative language is used.

Measure

The purpose of this step is to measure current process performance, compare it with the desired performance and collect relevant data about potential root causes of any existing gaps or unsatisfactory performance. Often, at this stage, we also generate a detailed process map.

A very easy approach to start this step is by using Solution Focus scaling questions. For example, 'on a scale from 1 to 10, where 10 represents your and your customers' hopes for the product or service and 1 is exactly the opposite, how would you rate the current performance?' You can follow this by asking 'Counters' and 'Resources' questions such as: 'What is already working well in this process?'; 'What is already enabling this good performance?' and so on. You can continue to use all the great Six Sigma analytical tools to identify patterns in the data you have collected; however, be mindful of which questions are guiding your analysis of the data. While finding where the process falls short or where gaps exist is the most common route of analysis, you can gain some surprising insights from understanding what happens when the process performs better than expected.

Examples of 'high performance' or 'positive deviances' are just as useful. Also, if you are analysing a process map, make sure the process map you are using is closer to the one I suggested in the last chapter (ie mapped to show the process when it works). Another commonly used concept at this stage is the 'Pareto principle', where we try to focus our attention on the 20 per cent of the variables or inputs that explain 80 per cent of the problem or variation. Instead, we can look for the 20 per cent 'positive core' that enables 80 per cent of the success.

Analyse

The purpose of this step is to identify, validate and select a root cause for elimination by analysing the data we have collected and by verifying cause-and-effect relationships. The analysis process should yield an identified root cause for the 'defect' under investigation.

The typical thinking behind the 'analyse' step is quite at odds with strength-based thinking. The terms used and the direction of inquiry are all very different.

However, nothing stops us from considering the 'positive core' of the process, which is the collective knowledge collected from interviews, themes of success and positive deviances to be our 'root cause of success'. This means that we should actively search for this positive core in order to understand it better and be able to expand it or build on it. This is where the practice of Positive Deviance with its emphasis on observing unusual cases of success comes in handy.

Otherwise, many of the analytical and statistical tools you already know such as T-tests and regression analysis can still be used, although the hypotheses you raise should specifically test generative factors, or factors you believe are supporting success rather than factors that drive defects. Also, if you are going to analyse the process in detail, why not use 'SMEA' (Success Modes Effects Analysis) for process analysis instead of 'FMEA' (Failure Modes Effects Analysis)?

Once you have identified the root causes of success, you can use Appreciative Inquiry to discover when these root causes were at their best and enabled the situation. This can then lead to a 'Dream' process where you imagine how good the process could be, if these enablers were present more consistently or to a larger extent.

Improve

The purpose of this step is to identify, test and implement a solution to the problem. Here your aim is to improve or optimize the current process by introducing changes that reduce or solve the impact of the identified root cause(s). The 'Improve' stage is actually where Appreciative Inquiry and Solution Focus can significantly contribute to the success of the project by enhancing the ability of the project team to implement a solution successfully. Some options include:

1 If at the last step you analysed and identified root causes of success and created a 'Dream' of what could be possible when

these root causes are fully utilized, you can now design the way forward using an inquiry around: 'implementing ideas successfully' or imagine 'What would be different once the solution is in place? Who would notice? How?' (Even if an actual solution is not yet known!)

2 Another approach would utilize the 'Scaling' and 'Small Steps' tools from Solution Focus by identifying what would be the quickest and smallest possible actions that could be taken right away to move the current process performance from N to N+1 on the scale. Following the 'Small Steps' process is aligned with Lean's value of 'failure proof' as the smallest steps we eventually come up with are normally very easy to implement!

3 You can also expand engagement levels towards the new ideas you now have by asking those involved with the process (or even its customers) what they appreciate about your ideas; when have they seen or experienced the identified root cause of success at work; and what would make the solution you are proposing even better?

4 Often, implementing new ideas takes some time and may require running a 'pilot' first. You can use Appreciative Inquiry and Solution Focus to reflect on your progress over time and thus maintain and increase the level of energy and enthusiasm towards it.

Control

The purpose of this step is to sustain the gains and monitor the improvements to ensure continued and sustainable success. Perhaps the word 'Control' is most at odds with the thinking behind many strength-based approaches. In a constantly emerging and changing world that is highly influenced by our conversations and changing understanding of reality, one can't actually achieve 'control' very easily. While many of us prefer to have predictable processes, we can actually expand the purpose of this step from 'control' to 'continued development' by inquiring appreciatively into our success so far and the changes we have implemented.

Another alternative is to introduce people involved with the process we have just improved to Solution Focus, Appreciative Inquiry or Positive Deviance so that they can continue to capitalize on their progress and successes. If team leaders are trained in being more appreciative of what works well and regularly spot best practices/ behaviours in order to affirm and replicate them, we are in full alignment of the Lean concept of *yokoten* (the practice of copying and using good ideas from one area to others).

5D

Readers who are more familiar with Appreciative Inquiry's 5D framework may wonder how to integrate Lean and Six Sigma with it. I have already highlighted, in Chapter 10, the opportunity of introducing Lean and Six Sigma principles at the 'Design' stage using them to guide the design and delivery of the ideas coming out of the Inquiry.

The Six Sigma VoC process can help identify factors that are critical to quality. These insights can be integrated with the internal conversations you have with stakeholders to define a more holistic, affirmative topic of inquiry (notice how this practice aligns with the Wholeness principle). These insights can enrich the conversation and help raise an even better topic than is otherwise discoverable.

Another option is to add some of the analytical tools from Lean and Six Sigma at the discovery stage of Appreciative Inquiry. The data analysis and the insights it generates (provided we take a strength-based approach to the analysis) can only enrich the insights generated through stories.

You can also introduce some of the ideas that are commonly followed at the Six Sigma 'Control' stage when working through the Deliver/Destiny stage of Appreciative Inquiry. For example, developing standards and documentation based on the best of what has been delivered can support the progress towards a better 'Destiny'.

Emerging new frameworks

Similar to the 'DCCA Framework' mentioned earlier, which emerged as a proposed new design at a recent workshop, I have come across another interesting thinking-framework that can integrate strength-based thinking with Lean Six Sigma. To the best of my understanding, it does not have a name yet so I will refer to it as the 'Needs-to-actions' framework. The process to follow is:

1 Identify the 'highest needs' – these are based on the needs of the customer, the organization and the people involved in the delivery of a product, service or process. You can use voice-of-customer or voice-of-business for that purpose.

2 Inquire into the 'best of today' – identify the best of what is known or available in the present. You can use Appreciative Inquiry Discovery, 'Counters' and 'Resources' from Solution Focus or an inquiry of examples of positive deviances.

3 New insights/new designs (and new needs!) – distil the insights from the last step through dialogue or analysis (or both). These insights will lead to new design ideas and possibly to the identification of new needs.

4 Action – take action based on the ideas from Step 3.

This is still a new and emerging idea but you can see how it integrates the two approaches nicely.

At the same time, remember that these standards and documents are useful on a temporary basis. To ensure continued development and a better destiny we should continue to develop the organization's 'appreciative eyes' and strength-based thinking. Doing so is a much better way to sustain and continue to develop the positive change. Otherwise, these standards and documents can easily be used from a deficit-based approach to highlight new gaps against them.

Summary

In this chapter I offered several additional possibilities for integrating strength-based approaches with Lean Thinking and Six Sigma. While you can definitely follow the ideas I proposed, you may already have your own unique ideas for such integration – ideas that could work better in your context.

By integrating strength-based thinking with Lean and Six Sigma processes, we actually create a significant change in emphasis, shifting from processes that put an emphasis on documenting and controlling to lighter processes that allow for more dialogue, learning and trust.

Having read this chapter, which approach are you compelled to try? Which frameworks are you familiar with? How can you add a different twist to them?

A proposed design for a strength-based Kaizen event

13

For many, participating in a Kaizen event is their first exposure to Lean Thinking as an effective way to deliver process improvement. The best English equivalent to the Japanese word *Kaizen* is 'positive improvement' or 'change for the better'. A Kaizen event (sometimes called a 'blitz' or a 'work out') is a concentrated, highly intensive activity designed to make rapid improvements quickly and efficiently. It typically takes between one and five days, and involves a dedicated, cross-functional team.

Kaizen events are excellent in demonstrating the impact Lean Thinking can have on processes by delivering rapid change. These events bring the Lean principles and a few relevant key tools to life while achieving a significant improvement to process performance – quickly! Good Kaizen events follow a rapid pace, keep their participants fully engaged and are full of energy!

Kaizen events come in many shapes and forms. No single Kaizen event is similar to the one before or after. Each practitioner has his or her favourite ways of preparing for, setting up and facilitating these events. Therefore, it is not easy to standardize them (and it actually may not add value to do so). If you have taken part in a Kaizen event or facilitated one, you will undoubtedly have your own unique experience to draw upon. You will probably also have several tools in your toolbox that you integrate into your Kaizen events based on the situation. As I show in the last chapter, many of these tools can be used with a strength-based approach.

The challenge of providing a standard design is even greater when applying strength-based lenses to Kaizen events, as this thinking is especially context-driven. Nevertheless, I am providing a suggested model here in the hope that it will be useful as a starting point for you to add to or build upon with your own preferences.

The Kaizen events I was introduced to and have facilitated had a relatively standard high-level design from which we deviated when necessary (by adding or taking out specific tools or tasks). It typically followed the structure shown in Figure 13.1.

FIGURE 13.1 The steps of a typical (deficit-based) Kaizen event

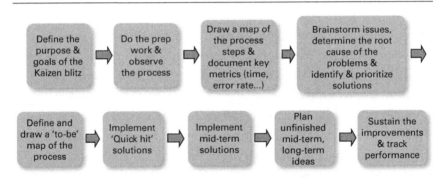

The strength-based version introduces several key components to this design. First, we add some of the key tools described in Chapter 11. The Strength-based Lean Six Sigma Tools – in particular the use of a strength-based process map. We also introduce an Appreciative Inquiry interview into the process 'at its best'. Finally, we use a strength-based and inquiry-focused interaction with all the stakeholders involved, right from the starting point all the way to the final evaluation. This is done by choice, specifically keeping in mind Appreciative Inquiry's Poetic, Anticipatory and Simultaneity principles.

The strength-based Kaizen follows the process shown in Figure 13.2.

FIGURE 13.2 The steps in a strength-based Kaizen event

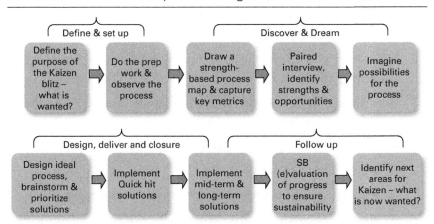

Note: many elements of the proposed design can be used as part of other improvement projects and are not necessarily limited to rapid improvement events.

The Kaizen 'define' stage

The purpose of this stage is to find out:

- Who is the customer for the desired change?
- What does the customer want to have happen?
- What strengths are already there?

In this stage we start establishing a useful platform for the desired change and provide an initial strength-based experience to the commissioning stakeholder(s).

Key questions you can ask your stakeholders at this stage are:

1 What do you want to achieve? Why is it important for you and for others?

2 On a scale of 1–10, how high is your desire to change the situation? What makes it so high?

3 If you could break down your (ambitious) goal, what would be the most immediate goal to focus on?

4 Who would benefit, and in what way, if you reach this goal?

5 How would you know that the Kaizen has been successful? What would be the first signs that things were improving?

6 What have you already tried so far to improve the process or situation? What worked well?

7 Who should be involved? How will you inform them and the rest of the organization?

   – Who can make a contribution to improving this process?

   – Who can be left out?

   – Who must not be left out under any circumstances?

   – Who are the people who influence the relevant organization or process?

   – Who should be a sponsor to ensure smooth progress?

   – Who should be a team lead?

8 What time frame should we set for ourselves to achieve success with this Kaizen?

9 What role would you want me (the consultant or internal resource) to play? What has been your best experience of…? (Complete according to the answer given.) How would you know that I was a useful resource for you?

10 Is there any important question that I haven't asked? What else is it important for me to know?

Setting up for success

The purpose of this stage

Successful Kaizen events depend on solid preparation and engagement from all stakeholders. In this stage we agree a date and duration for the workshop, identify a champion or sponsor (if that has not already been done) and nominate a team leader, as well as handling logistical requirements.

Key steps to complete:

1 SIPOC. (Identifying the process Suppliers, Inputs, high-level Process steps, key Outputs and relevant Customers.) We are using a SIPOC here as a conversational tool to enable the sponsor and his/or her nominated Kaizen team leader to agree the boundaries of the Kaizen event. There are other useful scoping tools that can be used for this purpose.

2 **Identify who should be in the room.** As the Wholeness principle tells us, it is a good idea to have the 'whole system' or a microcosm of the process in the room. In order to identify the relevant participants I either use the SIPOC we constructed earlier or the AREIN framework (Authority, Resources, Expertise, Information and Need). You may have your own useful framework to help identify relevant stakeholders.

3 **Ask the sponsor to complete and sign off a project charter.** The charter should include:

  - possibility statement, value proposition or a purpose statement for the event;

  - expected business and customer impact;

  - success metric(s);

  - who is the sponsor, the team leader and the improvement team;

  - timeline.

4 **Complete the required logistics.**

  - Book the venue, arrange meals/coffee breaks, entry badges or permissions and participants' accommodation (if needed).

  - Invite participants (normally done by the sponsor) and confirm attendance (handle any issues invitees may have).

  - Create a back-up plan for the operation or function (to cover for those attending your event).

  - Collect baseline performance data for the process and samples of good performance.

  - Finalize the agenda (taking into account normal work patterns that may impact on it).

  - Prepare training materials and training aides, (eg flip charts, paper, projector, office supplies, camera/video and a roll of brown paper.)

The big day has now arrived and the Kaizen event is starting. In this proposed strength-based design, I divide the Kaizen event into three parts. Each part has its own purpose and key steps.

The Kaizen event – Discover and Dream

Purpose of the Discover and Dream stages

The purpose of these stages is to frame the event from a strength-based view by mapping the process 'as is' (when it works well) and completing an Appreciative Inquiry interview to identify internal useful knowledge. Finally, we use 'dreaming' or other creativity processes to imagine the process as it could be when it is at its best.

The key steps are:

1 The opening by the sponsor provides the context, purpose and empowerment and introduces the team leader and facilitator.

2 The facilitator provides an introduction to the Kaizen concept and reviews the agenda, the team members introduce themselves and review the charter for the event. They also agree the ground rules to be able to work well together. It is particularly important to emphasize that this Kaizen event is using a 'different', strength-based approach to the improvement effort – especially for first-time participants being introduced to working with a strength-based approach (many are likely to expect a focus on problems and process weaknesses or waste).

3 Deliver a team-building exercise to introduce team members to each other and create a comfortable working environment. Use any exercise that you are familiar with that has worked well for you in the past.

4 Provide a training input (if required) – for example, an overview of the seven signs of Value; how to identify process customers; Lean principles and history.

5 If possible, 'go see' – in other words, view the process (ideally where it happens).

6 Complete an appreciative process interview in pairs/small teams – see Chapter 10 (appreciative interview for a process).

7 Complete a strength-based value-stream/process map:

- identify the steps in the process that add value to the customer (put a green sticker on the relevant process steps);
- identify strengths and opportunities for the process.

8 In small groups (or with the whole group, depending on the group's size) share some of the key insights from the interview and identify the 'positive core' – what enables the process to be at its best?

9 Consider asking the small groups to answer a 'future perfect' question – How would we notice if all problems were solved and the process was fully optimized? What would be the first signs? What else? Who else would notice? What would they notice?

10 Write a 'future statement' for the process describing the best this process can be.

11 Design, draw or build a prototype of the ideal state of the process and specify the desired results or hopes for the future.

12 Ask the group to identify, on a scale of 1–10, where the current process is in relation to the ideal state (10 being the ideal state and 1 being the complete opposite). It is absolutely okay for each participant to have their own view for this scale. Based on the number provided, ask the respondent to answer:

- If greater than 1 – what is already working well?
- If equal to 1 – has it always been '1' or have there been times when the process would have rated better? If so, what worked well then?
- If we were able to immediately improve the process to a slightly higher level on the same scale – what might be different then?

The Kaizen event – Design and Deliver

It is now time to build on all the useful information uncovered by the group at the Discovery stage, and the hopes for the future of the process by using some of the good ideas and the prototype of the future process. We start engaging the group in rapid cycles of small actions and regular affirmation of the progress made.

The key steps for the Design and Deliver stage are:

1 In teams – brainstorm ideas for immediate improvement:

- Small actions – what small steps would take us to the next step on the scale?

- Are these the smallest steps? What might be an even smaller step? What could be smaller still?

- Consider what is already working well or is available to take us further? How can we do more of what works?

2 Share your team's ideas for improvements.

3 Prioritize the ideas – use any prioritization technique you are comfortable with that is useful in the situation. It need not be too complex (for example, I use a simple two-by-two matrix drawn on a flip-chart paper with the axis being 'effort' versus 'potential benefit' or a simple 'sticky dots' voting process).

4 Ask the participants to form small teams to address the most useful and immediate actions, based on people's knowledge, past experience and energy. I sometimes introduce 'Open Space Technology' at this stage to help people self-select the actions they wish to pursue based on their energy, passion or interest.

5 Ask the participants to execute as many actions as possible over a short, defined time frame (for example 'the next two hours' or until the next lunch/coffee break).

6 At the end of each cycle of improvement gather the participants in their groups and ask them to value and affirm the progress made so far using some of the following suggested questions:

- What is progressing?
- What is better since the last time?
- How did you achieve that?
- What first signs of progress are already visible?
- What are you most impressed with so far?
- How can we take it to the next level?
- Where are you on a 'confidence scale' (from 1 to 10)? How confident are you that we are making progress? What is giving you this much confidence?

7 Continue the improvement work and progress affirmation in regular intervals. When a team completes the work on their chosen actions, ask them to self-select other improvement actions they are interested in pursuing.

8 Model or try the new process (this is an optional step that can be useful in identifying how well the new process is working and what would make it better still).

Closing the Kaizen event

All Kaizen events come to an end. Hopefully, at this stage, a significant improvement is noticeable and the participants feel energized about the progress they have achieved. Asking the group some of the following questions can help further cement the progress and deepen the positive relationships that have been established. These positive relationships will support the long-term sustainability of the positive outcomes.

Here are some useful questions to use at the closure stage:

1 What were you most impressed with?

2 What is already going well or better than before?

3 How is our 'future perfect' (or parts thereof) already happening?

4 Each participant completes a 'recognition exercise':

- Identify at least three things you were pleased to spot other participants doing.

- Over the next few weeks, recognize someone in the team for good actions, for providing extra value to the customer, or for a task well done.

The Kaizen event – follow up

Many Kaizen events can benefit from a follow up review of the progress achieved during and immediately after the event. The reason for doing so is to ensure improvements are sustained and further progressed.

Some useful steps to take at this stage include:

1 If any improvement actions or ideas remain open, complete as many of them as possible over a defined period (for example three to four weeks following the event). You can define this period with the sponsor, the team leader or the whole group.

2 Continue appreciating and affirming overall progress and individual contributions.

3 Document the progress made using pictures, articles, newsletters and so on, as relevant to your situation.

4 Measure the progress (using metrics and/or scale).

5 Hold a final valuation meeting. In this meeting you can:

- Conduct a valuation interview. This can provide you with some ideas for further future improvements. For an example, refer to the interview in Chapter 10 (the progress valuation interview).

- Plan the desired next steps – what is wanted now?

- Celebrate!

Summary

I hope you noticed the ways in which integrating strength-based approaches and tools in the Kaizen event can help the success of the event and raise the participants' level of engagement. My starting point was a Kaizen design that has worked well for me in the past. You may have your own preferred design. Feel free to introduce – and experiment with – the elements you liked the most or were particularly curious about from my design into your resulting unique design. You are invited to share your insights and successful experiences with us on our blog (www.almond-insight.com).

Moving beyond frameworks and tools

14

In the last three chapters I have offered many techniques and approaches to integrating strength-based thinking with Lean Six Sigma. I have introduced new applications for familiar tools, problem-solving processes and Kaizen events.

In Chapter 8 I talked about the importance of 'being' strength-based over 'doing' or 'thinking'. This compares with the classic application of Lean Six Sigma in which we normally prioritize it the other way around. In this chapter I would like to develop this point further by opening the door to a higher and more fluent level of practising Strength-based Lean Six Sigma – a level that is free of the focus on tools and processes. The way to get there is by developing our 'strength-focused eyes'.

Developing strength-focused eyes

It is perfectly possible to practise Strength-based Lean Six Sigma with the tools and processes I have introduced in this book. However, paying attention to *how* you notice what is happening around you, and using that information to interpret the world around you, is a great skill to have. Being able to view the situations you are facing from a strength-based point of view and to identify existing (albeit often hidden) strengths and possibilities is, in a metaphoric way, the difference between a 'green-belt' or 'black-belt' capability and the capability of a 'master black belt'.

Here are a few tips to improve your strength-based eyes.

Observing appreciatively

Observe and take notes of what works well (including cases of individual, team and organizational success). What is important to people in the organization? What strengths are available? What is wanted 'more of'? Where are their examples of positive deviants? What helps motivate people to move in a given direction? Being able to notice these elements and other similar ones through observations, targeted questions and dialogue provides the practitioner with a rich source of information and endless opportunities for possible steps to help people and their organizations move forward. You can find more examples of this skill in Chapter 17, which includes several case stories.

Another useful trick I sometimes employ is reflecting about 'what was not said' when the problem was described. This can provide useful directions for strength-based questions. For example, when a client tells me a problem occurs 'frequently', what is not said is when *isn't* the problem occurring!

Spotting generative topics for conversation and inquiry

The ability to maintain a strong focus on what is generative in each situation we're faced with, what is possible as a way forward and what 'gives life' to a given situation is immensely useful in being able to engage people in strength-based dialogue and positive action. For example, in Chapter 4, I described my experience with the Internet Service Provider in India where the clue for a useful direction towards a generative topic became apparent by pointing out the theme of 'commitment'.

This skill is also particularly useful when conversations turn in a deficit direction, as invariably happens. Finding the generative in the deficit helps create powerful shifts in our attention and energy. It also helps form different and useful strength-based questions. In situations like this, I prefer to ask, 'When is this problem not present? What happens then?' or 'When was the last time you last overcome this problem or a similar one? How did you do it?'

Taking the time to reflect appreciatively on the situations around us

Many of us are used to responding quickly to the events we're facing. Noticing strengths and positive shifts in a constantly changing environment and interpreting them appreciatively requires good practice and time for reflection. Taking time to practice this skill is a useful habit to acquire when we're faced with problems and issues. This is particularly important when experiencing change – either a change that we ourselves have planned through our improvement initiatives or changes that are driven through external factors.

Can you notice the highest moments during the experience? What did the people involved in the change learn from it? What would they wish for the future?

The ability to notice these strengths and better moments as well as reflect on them allows space for deeper insights to emerge.

Adopting a position of 'not knowing' – accepting that every situation is different

This is an important principle from Solution Focus. Every situation we face is new and unique, and should be treated as such, even if it is very similar to situations we have experienced before. We should approach every situation with a 'beginner's mind' and focus on the here and now. This will allow truly relevant solutions and ideas to emerge, instead of trying to fit the present situation into tools, processes and ideas that have been useful in past situations. Of course, there is nothing wrong in using your past knowledge and experience, but a better approach would be to ask for ideas from those who are affected by the current situation.

Developing your 'beginner's mind'

When you are called to support or work on an improvement project what do you do first? Many of us, almost immediately, and often without even noticing, start by making some assumptions and even potential work plans. Especially those of us who have developed an expertise in applying Lean Six Sigma and its various tools or processes, or in a specific operational area (for example, production, IT, customer services, etc). We are regarded as experts by others and the pressure may sometimes be high for us to find a solution to the problem. Often, your specific expertise means that you will assume that the current challenge is similar to past challenges, and you will therefore be tempted to use tools and processes that worked well before. Other times, if you are not sure of the potential solutions, you may reach out to other 'experts' for advice or conduct a research of 'best practices'.

Approaching a topic with a beginner's mind is actually a lot easier! All you need is your natural sense of curiosity, an idea for one or two strength-based questions you may want to ask the people involved (and even these questions may need to be changed when you are actually having the conversation). And finally, the last and most important ingredient of a beginner's mind: the ability to listen carefully and look for 'solution clues' in what you're hearing (rather than identify root causes for the problem). The clues for what is wanted (rather than what isn't), what is possible (rather than what isn't) and what resources and knowledge are available (rather than what needs to be introduced) are always there!

Keeping these key points in mind and practising them regularly will enable you to work with all the situations in front of you from a strength-based approach and to find or create the best tool or process to move forward.

Summary

This chapter provides guidelines that will enable you to go beyond practicing tools and processes. These tools will also help you to grow your ability to influence and lead positive change with people, organizations and processes.

This chapter also marks the conclusion of the fourth part of this book – the 'Design' part – in which we have explored and uncovered the best of 'what should be'. The 'best of what should be' is likely to include a strength-based application of some of the Lean or Six Sigma tools, or even a completely strength-based Kaizen event.

Before you move to the final part of the book, which will focus on taking further steps towards delivery of these ideas and a transformation of your process improvement initiatives, I invite you to reflect on the following questions:

1 How can Strength-based Lean Six Sigma tools, problem-solving processes or the proposed design for a Kaizen event help my organization or my clients?

2 What do I need to change or add to my favourite tools, problem-solving processes and the way I run Kaizen events?

3 What will these tools, processes and Kaizen designs enable me to do or achieve? What is their promise?

4 What stood out for me and invited me to try it?

5 In what ways do these practical ideas add value to everything I already do and know?

6 Who in my organization (or among the clients I work with) might be open to these new ideas?

7 To which existing activities in my organization can I easily add or introduce this approach or tools?

8 How can I develop my strength-focused eyes?

PART FIVE
Deliver/
Destiny

The final part of this book looks at the 'Deliver/Destiny' stage. The key underlining question at this stage is 'What will be?'

How do we implement the designs we have thought about and the hopes we have uncovered? How do we make it sustainable? Essentially, this is where 'the rubber meets the road'. How do we introduce the topic? What specific steps will we take with our clients or organizations? How do we ensure continuous improvement, sustainability and further expansion for Strength-based Lean Six Sigma?

Chapter 15 is the opening for this section and forms the start of 'Delivery'. In this chapter we explore effective and positive ways to introduce the topic of Strength-based Lean Six Sigma. What do we need to take into account and what options do we have? Chapter 16 shows you how to hold the initial conversation when an opportunity for a process-improvement project arises, in order to start well.

Chapter 17 will share a few case stories from practitioners around the world. I have collected some inspiring examples of different applications of Strength-based Lean Six Sigma. Each story shows a different way to work with strength-based change and Lean Six Sigma.

We close this part by moving into 'Destiny'. In other words, we are opening a door for the next generation of Strength-based Lean Six Sigma. What else is possible for this approach? How can we take it even further and deeper in the organizations we work with?

PART II

COLOUR

Introducing Appreciative Inquiry to organizations practising Lean Six Sigma

Lean Thinking and Six Sigma have been around for a long while (and the pursuit of quality and efficiency even longer). Many organizations have invested in building a Lean Six Sigma practice or have some experience in using these methodologies. The communities of practitioners are very large. By comparison, the practice of Appreciative Inquiry, Solution Focus and Positive Deviance within organizations has only started gathering pace. Therefore, you are more likely to come across leaders, managers and practitioners who have been exposed to Lean Thinking or Six Sigma, rather than those who have heard of or experienced strength-based change. Introducing your colleagues or clients to strength-based change or to Strength-based Lean Six Sigma and their potential benefits is therefore likely to be an essential starting point to practising them.

CASE STUDY Introducing Appreciative Inquiry
to a group of Lean Six Sigma experts – a case story

My first attempt at introducing and explaining Appreciative Inquiry to a
group of 12 peers happened a few years ago at my former corporate job.
All the people in the room were successful Lean Six Sigma Master Black Belts.
I was very new to Appreciative Inquiry and had just tried my first strength-based
intervention to solve a business challenge that my business unit had been
struggling with for years. The intervention went well and I wanted to tell others
about it, and about Appreciative Inquiry.

I gave the group an introduction to Appreciative Inquiry theory and principles;
I followed by facilitating a short paired-interview experience using these simple
questions:

- Tell me about the most successful business improvement activity (Kaizen,
  workshop, project, etc) you took part in:

  – What was your role?

  – How did you contribute to the activity's success?

  – What did others do?

  – What made it so successful?

- If you had three wishes for our group, what would they be?

After the interview I concluded with further details about 'how Appreciative
Inquiry works' and offered the opportunity for some Q&A. It all seemed to go well
and the energy in the room was noticeably higher as participants went through
the interview questions. Half the people in the room seemed to switch on to
Appreciative Inquiry and its potential applications, while the other half started
asking questions and raising challenges. They raised valid points that I didn't
expect and wasn't fully prepared for at the time. Their concerns centred on:

1 the potential of losing control over the change process due to the emerging
  nature of Appreciative Inquiry (not knowing up front where the process is
  leading to);

2 the length of time taken to conduct interviews, and whether this constituted a
  waste of time;

3 the potential defects in the process.

Additionally, the language I used in my presentation seemed to turn some people off.
Trying to explain social construction or multiple realities to Lean Six Sigma Master

Black Belts is certainly a dangerous feat! It took me a while to realize what was going on for some of the participants in the room. The members of this particular group were very good problem solvers who excelled at identifying defects and wastes in every environment! They were simply applying their usual line of inquiry to Appreciative Inquiry by looking for the defects and wastes in the process.

The key insights I gained from the experience were:

- The importance of trusting that the process will work. It is enough to provide a small experience (or more comprehensive if you have time) of the approach you wish to introduce (be it Appreciative Inquiry, Solution Focus or Strength-based Lean Six Sigma). Avoid the urge to explain it in the first instance. Allow your audience to reflect on their own unique experiences. Many Lean Six Sigma practitioners are naturally curious and want to break every process into its constituent parts, but doing so actually takes away energy and impact.

- Identify and keep in mind some of the potential benefits of strength-based change for your organization in case you are asked. It is useful to have a few ideas in mind of how your chosen strength-based approach can support what your audience is striving to achieve. (For example, how can it help improve business processes or reduce waste in the organization?) Highlight how it can help raise new ideas for improvement and greater commitment for change.

- To increase the level of comfort for your audience, you can also point out how some of the tools they know and are used to can still be used with a strength-based approach. This helps put your participants at ease, as they can build on what they already know.

I still consider this first experience as a high moment in my strength-based change journey. I share this story and my insights from the experience in the hope that it will help you to engage in more positive conversations with a unique population who can be a great support to the future success of any change initiative in organizations.

What is important to consider when introducing the topic?

Meet your client or the system you are working with 'where they are'

It is important to appreciate what they already have, even if it is a strong deficit mindset. Look for what is possible in the situation or with the group, and start there. By starting where your audience is, rather than where you want them to be, you are actually practising a strength-based approach. You are being appreciative of the current situation with all its possibilities, visible or hidden, well-planned or emergent.

Keep in mind that the reason Lean Six Sigma practitioners and advocates are so passionate about their methodology is, in its root, very strength-based: they actually hold a positive vision and a hope for what Lean Six Sigma can bring to organizations and their customers. Prepare some key phrases for people you will meet who may be wedded to their focus on what doesn't work – for the very best of reasons. Imagine what potential clients (internal or external) might feel, and prepare answers for them that respect and value their challenges and aspirations. Adopting this mindset is a truly appreciative way to practise.

Be clear in your mind and be prepared to answer why you would like to introduce a strength-based approach. What do you hope to achieve by introducing it? What value do you think it could bring? What will it help the system overcome or break through? This book should provide you with many ideas.

Believe in the participants, and in their ability to 'get it'. This can become a powerful vision for you as you prepare your introduction. Sometimes we get so focused on 'getting things right' and not making mistakes that we actually miss the simple hints of engagement and interest we can build on during delivery.

Some people will get it quickly whereas others may need to reflect on the experience and consider it in line with other knowledge and experience they have. For example, some business leaders I have met, especially business leaders who are visionary or have built their organizations and their career by using their and others' strengths, will feel at home with the strength-based approach. Others, especially those who prefer a very logical or rational explanation, may take more time.

Let go of what happens in the room. An important Open Space Technology (http://www.openspaceworld.org/) guideline states that what actually happens is the only thing that could and should have happened. Every conversation is different. Every conversation has its own energy, direction, pace and outcomes. You may never know what impact the questions you asked will have. If you are able to accept and respond to what *actually happens* in the room, you become an even better practitioner.

How to introduce: tips for success

Keeping in mind the Solution Focus principle advocating that 'every case is different', I can offer a few tips for a better introduction to the topic. You will still need to think of your own situation and take the steps that make most sense in your context.

The preferred method for adult learners is experiential learning. Therefore, assuming you will be presenting to adults, you need to focus on providing an experience of the approach. Theory, background details, explanations and even examples from elsewhere can wait for later. Focus on giving your audience an experience and make it relevant.

For example, the best way to introduce Appreciative Inquiry is by taking people through an actual interview experience first, without focusing too much on the theory and principles behind it. It is even better, if you can, to slightly tailor the generic interview questions to what this person or group are striving for, or to include their values. This will make the experience more relevant to them. In the case of Lean Six Sigma Green, Black and Master Black Belts, there are a few things that normally drive them to work in this area or with these methodologies:

1 Desire to make a positive impact on the business/customer experience/employees.

2 Curiosity – wanting to find a new idea/root cause or insight through analysing data.

3 A wish to bring better quality or improved efficiency to the organization.

4 A wish to teach useful thinking/analysis tools to others in the organization.

So, if you know what drives the person you are trying to engage with, you can craft impactful questions that will touch them deeply. That experience alone may drive their intellectual curiosity to research and learn more about the topic later. For example, if you ask a Lean Six Sigma practitioner about a time they were able to make a significant positive impact on their organization through the application of Lean Six Sigma tools, there is a higher chance they will connect with the experience than if you simply ask them about their 'highest moment' (such language may sound 'strange' to them).

This approach of tailoring generic questions is, by the way, true for anyone, not just Lean Six Sigma practitioners. As you prepare to introduce the approach, think about what your target audience cares about. What is their context? What challenges are they facing? Then craft questions accordingly to ensure that you tailor the language to fit the audience. Integrate their language and commonly used terms as much as possible. For example, in some situations, 'high moments' or 'high energy', or 'life-giving forces' in your questions are not the best terms to use. You may achieve a greater impact by asking for stories about experiences of success, delivering a positive impact, creating something new, achieving cost savings or delivering a unique contribution to the organization.

Another line of strength-based inquiry you could try is using a 'future perfect' question such as: 'Suppose our Lean Six Sigma programme achieved everything we hoped for and more, how would we notice? What would we see, hear or say that would be different? What would others notice? What would they say?' A future perfect question can provide you with many hints for possible next steps and indicate potential areas the group has energy to pursue. It may also surface topics to explore in future strength-based interventions.

In some cases, instead of delivering a presentation or a workshop about the strength-based approach, simply introducing a strength-based application with a tool your audience is either familiar with or already using, may help make the topic more comfortable and easier to grasp. The same applies to asking different, strength-based questions around key performance indicators, metrics or scorecards. This approach also follows the idea of providing experience as the optimal learning method.

Sometimes, especially when time is short, I use powerful metaphors as a way to convey the strength-based approach instead of an interview experience. One of my favourite metaphors is the 'cake metaphor'.

The cake metaphor is useful in describing the difference between classic Lean Six Sigma and Strength-based Lean Six Sigma in a language and imagery that is accessible and understood by many. Here is how I describe it:

If you imagine the entire operation or system to be like a giant cake, classic Lean or Six Sigma will focus on searching for and analysing the tasteless or unappetizing parts of the cake and look for ways to remove them. It may also look for why we used so much flour or chocolate, why it took so long to bake and why we set our oven to a particular temperature during the baking process. Could we have baked the cake with less flour, a shorter baking time or a lower temperature? We may even investigate why we left excess flour on the kitchen counter, how we used too many bowls and baking trays to make the cake and what materials or steps weren't necessary to reach the final outcome. We hope this line of inquiry will result in a better cake but, sometimes, the end result can be a shrunk, not fully risen or a runny cake (or we may have left 'holes' in it). It will certainly be a 'leaner' cake!

The Strength-based Lean Six Sigma approach is about finding, setting and keeping the best warm temperature so that our mix of flour, eggs, chocolate and sugar can become a tasty and attractive cake; it is about bringing in the best ingredients by focusing the attention on the tastier parts of the cake and seeking ways to expand them. It will ultimately result in baking a different, even tastier, whole cake (and more)!

I sometimes draw a cake on a piece of paper or flip chart to illustrate the idea, adding 'raisins' or 'berries' on top, depending on my taste on the day!

It doesn't matter too much what experience you provide, be it an interview, a strength-based tool or a conversation around a metaphor. If you make it a useful experience to the people you are working with, they will be able to gain fresh insights from the interview, the questions you ask, the tool you introduce or the conversation you facilitate.

Once you provide the experience of the approach, you can follow it by any of the following steps:

- Sharing a case story from this book. Was there a particular story that stood out for you or that may be relevant to the type of organization you work with?

- Talking about the value strength-based change or a specific approach can add to Lean Six Sigma initiatives in the organization.

- Exploring a concept, a thought or an idea for action you feel passionate about either through having read it in this book or from studying a strength-based approach to change.

- Developing and presenting your own vision or hope of how strength-based change can yield a successful outcome in the organization.

Finally, be ready for questions! The challenge often begins with the key strengths of most Lean Six Sigma practitioners: their natural curiosity and wish to understand the roots of anything in front of them. People who are used to solving problems, eliminating waste, finding and removing the root causes of defects and overcoming gaps may research Appreciative Inquiry from a deficit-based mindset. Or they may ask the presenter (who may not come from their area of practice) some challenging questions. The language and approach of 'classic' Appreciative Inquiry seems, on the face of it, to contradict what they know or are experienced in and comfortable with. Again, adopting their language and demonstrating the impact strength-based change can make *together with* or *in addition to* Lean Six Sigma is a good way forward. You may also be able to reframe some of the questions you get. Reframing can be a powerful experience on its own.

Summary

Knowing what could engage others with your topic and appreciating their unique skills and contributions can help you in designing your introduction to the topic and in crafting powerful strength-based questions that will be meaningful for your target audience.

Being appreciative and remaining patient when answering questions designed to expose possible weaknesses in your strength-based approach is essential and will ensure your audience stays engaged. If you are talking to Lean Six Sigma practitioners, anticipate potential negative (problem-focused) input, knowing that it is coming from a positive vision and strong conviction. You can reframe the message you're receiving by unlocking the hope hidden within the challenge. Always keep in mind that the people engaging with you on this topic could be strong partners and a force for positive change.

Once you have introduced the topic to a system, it may be the right time to explore potential areas for applying the approach and specific topics to work on. We will talk about that in the next chapter.

In the meantime, I invite you to think about the following questions:

1 Who do I want to introduce to Strength-based Lean Six Sigma?

2 What approach from the above ideas (or other equally good options) can I take to deliver an impactful introduction?

3 What questions can I introduce? What language will be most impactful?

4 What could my next step be?

Defining the topic of inquiry

The last chapter provided suggestions for ways to introduce strength-based approaches to change and to Lean Six Sigma into an organization. This chapter will help you take the next step of actually applying this approach to a particular area of an existing process challenge or an improvement opportunity.

There is a well-known Chinese proverb which states that 'all great journeys begin with the first step'. In the case of strength-based change in general, and Strength-based Lean Six Sigma in particular, the proverb should probably read 'all great strength-based changes begin with the first question'. The first question asked is very important. As Marilee Adams (1998) points out, our questions can lead us down the 'learner path' or the 'judger path': the consequences of each path are very different. The first is likely to generate solutions and a change for the better, while the other may yield blame and despair. In addition, Appreciative Inquiry's principle of Simultaneity tells us that change begins with the first question we ask.

More specifically, when we are called in to apply our process-improvement skills to a given situation, our first few questions influence the people we interact with and the choice of topic we will focus on. It is very important to consider carefully the questions we ask: many of us, successful process improvement agents, were trained in methodologies that naturally lead us down the 'judger path'. The more affirmative the questions are, the better, as they are likely to lead us towards a topic that is engaging to work with, a topic that 'gives life' to people and supports them in their change efforts towards a more positive direction.

TABLE 16.1 Examples of reframed topics

Initially proposed topic (The problem we wish to fix/reduce/move away from)	Generative topic (What we want to have more of, to expand or grow or move towards)
Reducing the costs arising from train delays due to faulty carriages exchanged incorrectly	Using our expertise in successfully exchanging carriages to improve our performance
Reducing customer complaints	Perfect connections
Reducing lost baggage	Perfect arrival experience
Eliminating waste in processes	Discovering what is value-add and important to our customers and to us
Reducing errors in order processing and delivery	'Perfect orders' – the right order, at the right time in the right place

Time and time again, I have experienced the difference a switch from a typical topic to a truly generative topic makes. The difference is often visible and audible. People are simply more attracted to, engaged with and curious about a generative topic than they are with a more standard topic. Table 16.1 provides a few examples.

Arriving at the right generative topic depends on a mix of knowledge and skill in asking generative questions. The 'art of identifying the topic' becomes easier and more straightforward with experience. Often when we arrive at a topic that sits well with our audience (be it a project sponsor, a process operator/owner, or a leader in the organization), we can see the change in body language as well as the more enthusiastic tone of voice that comes from a greater level of interest, passion and engagement.

How to uncover great topics

Almost all my process-improvement conversations with clients (a client may be from within your organization or an external client) begin with a detailed description of the problematic present and its root causes. Clients have normally thought through and carefully analysed the situation and have a very good story to tell about the situation, why they have arrived there and everything they have already tried in order to solve the problem that didn't work. Often I hear a lot about what is not wanted or what they wish to reduce or eliminate. Rather than engage in conversation at this stage or try to understand the problem in detail (as I used to do in the past), it is important to listen very carefully and look for cues about what is actually wanted. The cues are normally there although not always clearly expressed. I believe that by helping the client identify what they actually want *instead of* the problem I am already helping them start the shift in that direction. It can be useful to use Solution Focus or Appreciative Inquiry questions to help the client reframe their view of the situation. For example:

1 I understand that you really do not want to have X (the problem) here; what would you like to have instead?

2 Suppose we found a solution to X, what would we have here instead?

3 I understand that many things are going wrong here (giving some examples). What is most important for us to get right?

4 Are there situations when X is not happening? What is happening then instead?

5 When has this area performed at its best? What was happening then?

Often the answers to these questions help me identify the first few cues leading towards *several* different potential topics. Note that at this stage there are indeed several different potential topics rather than just one. In other words, the absence of (or a solution to) a given problem may be expressed in several different ways rather than just one way.

After carefully listening to these cues, I can intervene by asking 'So, you want to have more of Y?'

'Y' in this case may be a combination of a few of the cues I have received from the answers to my questions. The answer to this new question often helps the client further develop what they want to have instead of the problem or the answer may indicate that something else rather than Y is wanted.

In some cases, the topic that the client arrives at, while better and more wanted than the problem we started with, is still not as engaging for them as it could be. The cues are often in the body language and tone of voice. If this is the case it is important to inquire: 'What might make the situation even better (than just having Y)?' and 'What else would make it better?'

Another approach that can help the client reframe a problem statement and arrive at a generative topic is to draw a little diagram on a piece of paper or a flip chart:

TABLE 16.2 Advancing from Not Good to Good, Better and Great

Not good	Good (status quo)	Better	Great
Having problem X (as described by the client)	Not having problem X	Having Y	Having Y and...

The topic definition conversation should continue until an engaging, generative and exciting topic is arrived at that describes what is wanted and how the situation would be better when it is reached. In essence this topic is the 'seed dream' that describes what is wanted and will later develop into other, greater possibilities for discovery. This process of exploration may require some time.

In some cases, the initial conversation and topic identification happens with one person in the organization who initiates the conversation (typically, a leader in the organization, a project sponsor, or a project leader). It is always a good practice to confirm the topic you have arrived at by exploring it further with other stakeholders (for example, operators, project team members, customers) to reach a consensus for a final topic that is considered generative by all. It is best to have everyone involved in the room from the beginning and to arrive at the topic together as a team. However, if it is not possible to have everyone in the same room for this topic exploration, you can still reach a final agreed topic by either:

1 taking the other stakeholders through the same process of inquiry as detailed above; or

2 introducing the topic you have already arrived at during your initial exploration and asking questions such as: 'What do you find attractive in this topic?'; 'What is important to you about the topic?'; 'What, in your view, could make this topic even better?'

Essentially, the more the topic is generative and widely agreed as describing a shared hope, wish or an aspiration for the current situation, the better. The topic has to describe where the system wishes to move towards rather than what it wishes to move away from.

Creating a platform for change

So now that you have the topic for inquiry, you may ask yourself, what's next? How to progress from here? Some of us get very excited after the topic is identified. So much so, that we would like to carry on straight away with applying our strength-based process-improvement skills or the discovery inquiry to the topic. My suggestion instead is to follow the topic selection with establishing a 'platform for change'. The platform is a particularly useful concept from Solution Focus. Time spent building it at this stage will pay great dividends later.

Before I describe the platform-building process in detail, it is important to clarify that the platform I refer to *is not* what is commonly known as 'the burning platform' from John Kotter. In fact it is quite a different concept!

So what is the platform?

Imagine the change your client wishes to have is like a building. In order for the building to be well-built and remain stable, it needs strong foundations. The foundations of this building (which represents the change the client wishes to have) are essentially the platform you will be building together.

The platform starts with identifying the topic, or what both parties wish to work towards. It then identifies who wants to move towards this direction and why. What is the benefit they will get by reaching there? Identifying many stakeholders in the organization who want to move in the direction you have identified helps create strong support for the project. If no one, or only few, in the organization would like to move towards the future as described in the topic we identified, then there is simply not enough support for the change to succeed.

The next area to explore is what would support the client in moving towards the topic. In other words, what would enable the organization and its people to move in the direction that is outlined in the chosen topic? For example, what resources, skills, know-how or expertise, connections, leadership support and unique gifts exist that have been useful in solving problems before, and can be used in our current project?

Another useful question is: 'How will you know progress has been achieved? What would be the first signs?' This question is important as it provides clues or potential metrics you can refer to later to check that you are moving in the direction you wanted to.

At this stage it is good practice to check with the client to see if he/she is confident that you can both achieve success. This is a useful point at which to reflect on their level of confidence, now that you have uncovered some resources and know what the first signs of success would be. Explore in detail what enables them to be so confident already and what would increase the level of confidence even further. The answer will give both you and the client ideas about what they can do to further increase the chances of success.

Finally, great projects often benefit from having an attractive symbol or image associated with them, or perhaps a catchy slogan/ tag line: sometimes they have both! A useful way to arrive at a symbol or image is to explore relevant metaphors. I like to conclude the platform-building process by identifying the symbol or slogan that further helps people engage with the inspiring topic we have selected.

Et voilà! Your platform is now solid and you can start working on the process-improvement project you've identified with greater confidence!

Summary

The two most important first steps when embarking on a strength-based project are: 1) identifying the topic you both wish to move towards; and 2) building a platform for change. In this chapter I have shared with you my preferred way to do both. The suggestions I provided were meant to be starting points from which you should be able to develop your own unique ways of embarking on process-improvement opportunities from a strength-based approach. There are good processes and tips for doing this, but some of it is a matter of 'art' and of expressing your own unique way of asking 'questions that matter' which help move people forward.

Where do you move on to from here? Since each project and each situation is different, you will have to choose the tools, processes or approaches that you think can be most useful in moving forwards from this point. These may come from topics I have presented in this book, insights you gained through reflecting on my questions or your own unique knowledge and experience, as well as your comfort with the different strength-based approaches. However, by identifying the topic and by establishing the platform, you can rest assured that you have taken the first few steps in this 'great journey'.

In the next chapter I collect a few case stories from other practitioners that further demonstrate the value a strength-based approach brings to process-improvement initiatives through Lean Six Sigma. They may also provide you with inspiring ideas that could be relevant to your projects.

Strength-based Lean Six Sigma case stories

T hroughout the book, I have shared examples of my own experiences in applying a strength-based approach to Lean Six Sigma. In this chapter, I will share case stories that were provided by colleagues from around the world. Each story is a unique experience of Strength-based Lean Six Sigma; each practitioner has applied their own knowledge and ways of working to the situation at hand. Together these stories highlight the variety of applications and the global reach of this emerging practice.

In the first story, 'From Crisis to Global Competitiveness: Learning from a Spectacular Journey,' Henrik Kongsbak from Denmark, an experienced consultant specializing in organizational development and leadership training, describes a success story of how a manufacturing facility for medical devices in Denmark transformed itself from being unwanted and destined for closure to 'Most Wanted', and then to 'Best in Class' over a three-year period using Appreciative Inquiry together with Lean.

This story powerfully illustrates the Positive and Simultaneity principles: the consultant helped the client reframe from what they wanted less of, to what they truly wanted. It shows the power of generating a positive vision through Appreciative Inquiry as a way to engage a whole operation in a Lean Six Sigma initiative. It also teaches us much about sustaining momentum for change in the face of uncertainty, as it was two years before the facility was awarded the manufacturing of a new product.

CASE STUDY From crisis to global competitiveness: learning from a spectacular journey – by Henrik Kongsbak

NovoLet Production, part of Novo Nordisk, the world-leading provider of insulin for diabetics, had been producing the first Novo Nordisk blockbuster injection devices for more than 15 years. However, as times changed, new products in the pipeline were ready to replace NovoLet. Additionally, globalization made it difficult to compete against low-cost countries. The production facility was destined for gradual closure, following the withdrawal of the NovoLet pen from the market.

The situation created a very negative ambiance at the production facility: employees felt betrayed and left out; commitment dropped and absenteeism rose as the level of trust between management and employees deteriorated.

The management had been told to reduce absenteeism by 50 per cent, which was the determining reason for inviting us in (Henrik and a colleague). Arriving at the first meeting with management and a representative from the employees, we knew little about the journey we would be travelling together. Having talked about the reason for inviting us, we started to ask strength-based questions, like: 'If absenteeism is your problem, what would you like instead?'

These questions started to shift the focus from the perceived problem to the desired outcome and opened opportunities for more optimistic thoughts about how they could raise commitment and thereby reduce absenteeism. When we asked the question, 'If, as a production facility, you were an ultimate success in two years, what would you have accomplished?', we got to the heart of the matter.

The answer was, 'If we were an ultimate success, we would have been able to raise performance so much that we could attract a new product.' Everybody around the table nodded and that became *the focus* of the project rather than absenteeism. Over the course of the next few months, we put together a project where we involved all 130 employees as well as other relevant stakeholders (about 20) in a process of what it would take to attract a new product.

The process

A two-day workshop with management served to introduce them in more depth to the principles, processes and tools behind Appreciative Inquiry, as well as allowing them to define a 'burning desire'. We needed a burning desire that pinpointed the ambition and emphasized the benefit for everybody. On the second day, a team leader, Carsten, came up with 'Most Wanted' as our ambition. Everybody nodded instinctively, and it became a burning desire for the project that served several purposes. First, it pinpointed the ambition about being most wanted as a future supplier. Second, it emphasized how we wanted to make every employee most wanted in case we didn't succeed with our overall ambition of attracting a new product. Third, it had a humorous touch that we believed would have a good effect. Finally, it is associated with the 'wild west' attitude of 'let's take things into our own hands'.

During the two days, the management team also worked on applying the strength-based approach to their normal ways of working by working through the following questions:

1 How can we approach problems and barriers as opportunities?

2 How do we approach breakdowns and failures as learning opportunities?

3 How do we approach employees who we believe are not delivering in a strength-based and appreciative way?

Last but not least, we discussed how we could make this project *everyone's* project, not just a management- or consultant-driven project. From the start, we agreed that we had to involve a sample of people in a similar process, not only with the ambition of being Most Wanted but also in the process of how we should involve our colleagues and stakeholders. We decided to have another two-day workshop with a working group.

Tough but necessary conversations

The two-day workshop that followed, with a representative group of employees, was both challenging and productive. We all knew that setting an ambitious goal in a production facility that was going to close, and where trust and morale was low, wasn't going to be easy. However, the management team was determined after the first workshop, so we were ready to face some tough yet necessary conversations. And we did! Several people were, at best, sceptical about the whole idea of raising ambitious goals, but on top of that, doing it by 'being positive' seemed to many 'fluffy and weird'. However, the two days gave room for some honest and tough discussions, where the whole group came closer to understanding each other's intentions, dilemmas and aspirations. At the same time employees found out how serious the management team was about this project, and management learned how to make this everyone's project. We left the seminar illuminated, closer and with an emergent foundation of mutual trust.

The core-group workshop was followed by a one-day summit for the whole production facility, including relevant stakeholders and suppliers, in total about 140 people. Having only one day, we focused on two areas:

1 creating an atmosphere where hope and action could connect;

2 setting a very short time frame for improvements, thereby having the summit serve as a kick-start to their quest for being most wanted.

Preben, the head of the production facility, invited everybody to join by presenting the Most Wanted ambition, and openly declaring that he didn't know how to get there. He noted that 'collectively, we have 984 years of experience in making these devices, so let's find out what we do when we're at our best and what we can do to do better'. The conversations started with paired interviews that focused on peak experiences as well as best improvement ideas. In many ways, it was a slow start, but learning from their peak experiences raised the participants' confidence as they recalled spectacular previous accomplishments in the midst of their perceived downturn. Generating improvement ideas made everybody aware that they were among a group of colleagues who had plenty of ideas about how to improve. Energy and hope increased as people realized that being Most Wanted might be ambitious – but not necessarily *impossible*.

The summit was a turning point in the process of becoming Most Wanted. As Preben and his management team noted afterwards, 'It was as if the old atmosphere had evaporated and a new one emerged. We had regained trust in one another, and we felt like a team, and when you do that things start happening.'

Building on momentum

Following on the summit and in order to build on the momentum it created, we engaged every work shift in a half-day workshop at the production facility under the headline 'Do it Now'. Every work shift was engaged for three hours in brainstorming, prioritizing and executing small improvements that could make them Most Wanted. This was combined with the implementation of Kaizen (a part of their Lean efforts) aimed at creating small yet visible improvements that would be clear signs of progress. This approach was used later when employees suggested a one-week workshop to calibrate production lines that would allow them to produce more smoothly and with fewer storage buffers. Previously, three experts had worked for 18 months on this problem without success. This time the employees accomplished it in a week while still meeting normal production. This meant reducing storage requirement from 1,500 to approximately 100 square meters, and reducing cycle time by 80 per cent.

During the process of applying this radical, high-involvement and strength-based approach, the management team met at least once a week to share and discuss ways in which they could address problem-oriented issues using strength-based methods. This helped them apply the new way of working to their everyday challenges, thereby staying focused.

TABLE 17.1 The process of embedding Appreciative Inquiry principles at NovoLet Production

Step	Purpose
Two-day management workshop	Management defined their burning desire, made a plan to engage the plant and were introduced to appreciative leadership.
Two days core-group workshop	A representative group of employees was introduced to Appreciative Inquiry and discussed how to engage the entire plant in becoming Most Wanted.
One day Whole System Summit	The whole system, including main stakeholders, created hope for the future and short-term improvement actions.
Half-day 'Do It Now' workshops	Each shift brainstormed, prioritized and executed small actions to become Most Wanted.
Weekly management meetings	Embedded addressing problems in a strength-based way (Appreciative Lean culture).

The results

The impact of the Most Wanted process was profound. Over a period of four months productivity per employee rose by 44 per cent and cost per pen declined by 25 per cent. Over a period of two years, while they were gradually phasing out the product, they achieved the following results:

1 The cost per pen was reduced by 17 per cent, while volume dropped by 21 per cent over the same period of time.

2 Cycle time was reduced by 80 per cent.

3 Deviations from quality standard requiring corrective actions were reduced by 90 per cent.

4 Employee satisfaction survey results increased from 3.6 to 4.37 (on a scale from 1 to 5).

5 Engagement survey results increased from 3.48 to 4.08 (on a scale from 1 to 5).

6 Customer complaints decreased by 10 per cent.

7 The Most Wanted process was graded 'excellent' in an internal assessment within the categories 'working environment' and 'business plan' (the first time in seven years that the assessors had given this grading).

8 NovoLet Production was appointed 'Best in Lean Leadership' in its production division.

9 And absenteeism? It was cut in half – from 12 per cent to 6 per cent.

These results convinced top management that NovoLet should be given the start-up of Novo Nordisk's new product, a remarkable accomplishment that has been acknowledged both within Novo Nordisk, as well as in the industry in general. Today, visitors from other parts of the company, as well as from other companies, come regularly to study how NovoLet combines a hard results-driven focus with an appreciative mindset.

In 2009, the Most Wanted process entered a competition organized by the Danish Management Board. Among more than 40 other change projects in all fields of consultancy, including strategy, management, sales and Lean, Most Wanted was awarded the Best Change Project of the year.

From Most Wanted to Best in Class

During the next 18 months to the end of 2010, the management team worked on both setting up the pilot production facility as well as phasing out NovoLet. This required a new burning desire process that was called 'Best in Class'. The new product also marked a new sourcing approach for production that allowed sourcing from other continents. As part of the Best in Class focus, the management team invited Henrik and his colleague to engage everyone in defining and setting the ambition for the new task. The new process has been at least as successful as the previous one, and Device Manufacturing Production (DMP), as they are now called, continues to improve. The Business Unit (to which DMP belongs) has adopted Best in Class and has set out to win a global manufacturing excellence award by 2014.

Learning and reflections

The process had several interesting learnings, one of which has been how to apply a seemingly simple learning philosophy such as Appreciative Inquiry in

FIGURE 17.1   The journey from Most Wanted to Global Excellence

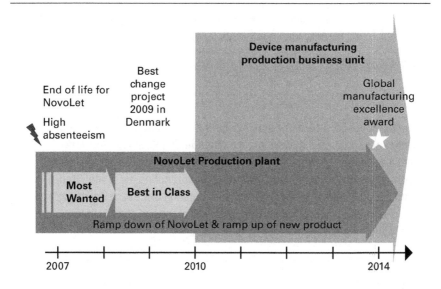

a complex and very problem-oriented production facility. Involving the whole organization in a strength-based process is a well-proven aid. However, Appreciative Inquiry and other strength-based approaches had to be combined with Lean Six Sigma to be able to address everyday work that is mainly focused on handling problems, eliminating barriers and securing a smooth production flow.

Classic Lean Six Sigma has been successful in developing specific tools to address crucial issues in a production environment, but are all based on deficit-thinking. At NovoLet Production, employees and managers have developed their own Strength-based Lean tools, which are now part of the way they run their production. An example is the fishbone diagram that is used to analyse positive deviances in the same way as errors and breakdowns (for more detail on this tool refer back to Chapter 11).

We have been asked many times how the production facility managed to keep the momentum over more than two years before they were awarded the production of the new product. For the management team this was never an issue. As they said, 'We just needed to ask how we could do even better.'

Having said that, the management team did several things. First, they worked hard to find ways of talking about problems and breakdowns in a strength-based way. Second, they constantly worked on small improvements, and encouraged and pursued ideas for improvements from their employees (including ideas that they themselves didn't consider to be important), thereby underlining everyone's importance and the importance of everyone's ideas. Third, they made improvements very visible by having key performance metrics visible for all. Fourth, successes were celebrated by all, and the teams and individuals who accomplished them were always acknowledged.

But probably most important, they successfully kept open an honest dialogue with employees, thereby leading through honesty, integrity and openness.

Henrik Kongsbak has more than 12 years of experience as a consultant within organizational development and leadership training. His work focuses on how groups and individuals reach solutions faster and with more commitment using strengths-based approaches. He is affiliated with several MBA programmes and is a founding partner in Resonans A/S. For more details contact Henrik on hk@resonans.dk or visit his company's website www.resonans.dk.

Jeremy Scrivens is an Australian consultant who uses Appreciative Inquiry together with Process Improvement techniques with his clients. This second story, taken from his experience, demonstrates further how a change of direction in what the consultant inquires into at a client system, results in several internal solutions and 'know-how' being rediscovered, thus generating higher level of engagement for a Lean initiative.

CASE STUDY   The story of adaptive change in Blue Sky Catering – by Jeremy Scrivens

A leading in-flight caterer, Blue Sky Catering, took over the operations of a major competitor. The new CEO, Robert, was concerned that many of the staff he had inherited appeared to lack motivation and passion for their work. Robert asked Jeremy to undertake a diagnostic survey to find out what was wrong, what the gaps and problems with the culture were and the 'root causes' of employee disconnect.

The word 'diagnostic' actually means looking for what is diseased! At the time I saw this as a great opportunity to apply the full power of my sophisticated problem-identification toolset and bring them back to the executive board table – so I did. I interviewed 60 cooks, chefs, drivers, dishwashers and tray assembly workers and asked them what they didn't like about their jobs and working at the company – after all, it was important to get to the root cause of the problem, so I had been taught.

So they told me – stories about workers stealing the bonded liquor, stories of poor-quality food going out to the aircraft, stories complaining about upstream suppliers who didn't have the ingredients or the equipment ready on time.

They told me all the 'D stories': stories of disruptions, deficits, disconnects and delays and of overall broken customer processes. Their stories covered all that I had been taught in my process improvement training and textbooks. There was little love lost between different areas of the facility. The chefs didn't talk with the assembly workers, who in turn left the food they plated in holding fridges to be picked up by drivers, who walked across no man's land to collect the food but did not speak to assembly workers.

I was so excited: this was the best, most comprehensive diagnostic I had ever done. I couldn't wait to share all these wonderful problems with the executive team. I was really earning my money! So I went back up to the board room and did just that. By the end of two hours, everyone in the room was totally demoralized, dismayed and de-energized.

Then one executive cried out 'Don't we ever do anything well around here?' At that point my mind flashed back a few years to a presentation I had seen about Appreciative Inquiry, an emerging paradigm on focusing business change conversations and on discovering and building on what works, not what is broken. The penny dropped for me. I persuaded the CEO, Robert, to let me go back to the facilities and re-interview the staff. This time I would focus on finding and bringing back stories of what worked for people: stories of peak engagement, great processes and results, even if this wasn't the norm.

This time, we got the positive stories. Stories like the one from the staff member, Mike, who had been working the dishwasher. Mike said that the time he had felt most engaged was 10 years before, when he could see and talk to the next person on the dishwasher who took the plates that Mike loaded onto the conveyor belt. Mike could see this person and talk to him, so he was connected socially with another human being.

But what had the company done in the 10 years since Mike said he had been emotionally engaged with his work? They had bought in new equipment that automated part of the process, reducing the number of operators and separating them spatially, all in the name of efficiency and automation. No one had asked Mike what should be done… Mike could no longer see his mate on the dishwasher and his performance slipped. Mike said, 'I would love to work with another operator again and have someone to talk to; I wouldn't get distracted and make so many mistakes.'

Then there was the story from Jill, who led the Plating Assembly Team, who said that she basically came to work, did her bit and then went home. She actually ran a successful part-time home catering business outside of work but said she came to work at the catering company to make some extra money. I asked her if there had ever been a time when she felt that she had been using her business talents at work. She said only one time in four years, but she remembered it well:

It was a weekend, I was on a shift and all the managers were away on some sort of training course. We only had a skeleton staff and then we got a call to say that a flight on route from Christchurch to Jakarta had been forced to divert for emergency repairs. It was due to land in two hours and the airline had put in an urgent request for meals for 150 passengers.

Even though the airline had no current contract with us, we wanted to help. But what should we do here? There were no managers around and no menus to work from – this was a manager's business, wasn't it? No one on the ground floor was authorized to create menus.

But Jill and the other team leaders really wanted to help the stranded airline passengers – compassion was an important value to them. So Jill got the other team leaders and members together and in 30 minutes the whole team had created a meal menu from what was available in the fridges. They pulled together as one team to cook, assemble and load the trucks with the meals.

All demarcations and current processes were forgotten as they worked together. They shared tasks: the assembly team went out on the truck with the drivers to help load the plane, but also to explain to the flight attendants what was in the menu. This was unheard of: assembly people weren't allowed to go out on the trucks, it wasn't in the process! This was the first and only time that the people who prepared the food got to speak to the flight attendants – the people who served the food – in real time.

One week later, the airline sent a letter of thanks to the company CEO saying that this was the best customer service they had ever experienced from any caterer. Six of the eight staff interviewed in the catering unit brought up this story as their best experience of working at the company and asked if they could experience it again – could they please get to own what they created more of the time?

When the executives heard this and the other positive stories, you could have heard a pin drop in the room – it was a powerful moment. A decision was taken at that meeting to pull a project team together comprising people on the ground floor to design new Lean work processes that enabled people to engage with their work and their customers more frequently. The project transformed the culture and the results in the company, which was later sold to another company. The journey that started in this project continued and expanded into the European Operations.

Jeremy Scrivens is a consultant, speaker and author who works with commercial, government and not-for-profit organizations. His work focuses on whole-system change through Appreciative Inquiry and strength-based business improvement to enable greater performance, innovation, engagement and well-being. He has recently contributed to the ARK Group's prestigious 'Business Process Management' published in London in 2012. For more details contact Jeremy through: emotionaleconomy.net@gmail.com or visit his company's website: http://www.theemotionaleconomyatwork.com.

The next story comes from the United States. In it Ankit Patel, an independent consultant, demonstrates the value of including an Appreciative Inquiry process with a technical problem-solving process based on classic Lean Thinking. He explains how Appreciative Inquiry helped identify additional ideas for improvement and establish a strong sense of commitment towards changing the situation for the better.

CASE STUDY   The appreciative way of implementing a lean communication process – by Ankit Patel

A producer of colouring pelts for plastic products asked me to support their improvement efforts. Initial conversations with the plant manager were followed by data collection to identify areas for improvement. In an open forum with all the employees, I asked three questions to guide my analysis:

1 What is the one area of the plant that, if fixed, would make things hum?

2 What is the one thing you would like to see changed in your operations?

3 What are your ideas on how to make your job easier?

The responses revolved around a common theme of 'communications'. The challenges raised were around lack of communication or miscommunication. To add to the complexity, a large portion of the workforce was of Hispanic origin: many could not speak English well or even at all. The first action we decided to take was to improve the communication between the three shifts in the plant.

I designed a two-day intervention with representation from all shifts. The representatives were all supervisors or respected individual contributors. The first day, designed to focus on a problem-solving approach, was supposed to lead us to creating a standardized daily management process with improved communications. The second day was dedicated to an Appreciative Inquiry process around the topic of 'flawless, effective and connected communication'.

The agenda for the first day included a discussion aimed at clarifying and reframing everyone's understanding of communications (what is valuable about it; what activities are involved; what connections are needed; how communication flows), as well as communication exercises. We mapped the current communications process and created a 'to-be' version for the desired-future process. We hoped to be already trying some of the changes at the end of that day.

The agenda for the second day started with paired Appreciative Inquiry interviews, consolidation of the information from the interview in groups of between six and eight participants and identification of the 'positive core', the guiding themes for positive communications and desired provocative propositions. We planned to integrate the provocative propositions with the to-be process from the first day to create an improved second version. The next step was going to be determining the required actions, the owners of those actions, and the timelines, along with a governance structure. At the end of the event we included time to debrief with the plant manager and other leaders to obtain their approval.

What actually happened

We started the first day with basic introductions and then quickly moved into Lean training, which was centred on how to see value and waste, and how they relate to communications. Straight away I sensed that there were overt tensions between people in the room, as well as tension due to the fact that the leadership *wasn't* in the room. I decided to keep to the plan, and focus on learning and problem solving. I did not want to focus on addressing the interpersonal concerns at that stage so I decided it was out of scope.

Even though addressing the interpersonal relationships issues was out of scope they kept surfacing. Participants commented that, 'There are some people who just don't respect anyone else' and 'I don't know how we can operate this way if people [ie leadership] don't respect us.'

At the end of the first day I had decided to bring in the plant manager and senior manager to have a discussion about the cultural issues – this was not planned in advance but I felt it was essential. The meeting started off with the group reporting what we had accomplished through the Lean training, mapping the current communications processes and designing a communications meeting for each shift that would be supported by a visual aid board. Quickly, the conversation shifted to the cultural and interpersonal issues. As a result, heated arguments were raised. At one point a member of the team pointed his finger at another member who had been working with him all day and said, 'It's your fault we are having these problems'.

My hunch was that he really meant to say it to the senior manager but decided to pick another, safer, target. Shortly thereafter the meeting was adjourned. Everyone left for the day. At this point I felt overwhelmed – I was unsure of how to deal with the situation the group was in. I was confident I could deliver the process necessary to address shift communications, but I knew it would not address the fundamental issues that would prevent the process from taking off.

We started the second day by reviewing the outputs from the first day. I then paired team members for Appreciative Inquiry interviews. I decided to pair participants whom I felt didn't have a relationship or had a tense relationship. The topic for the inquiry was 'flawless, effective and connected communication'. The topic was further defined as follows:

> Flawless, effective and connected communication is when you communicate to another person where everything is in sync. It's a time when you and the other person are on the same page and the communication is almost effortless. Sometimes the communication may even seem unconscious.

We asked participants to share high-point experiences of personal communication as well as experiences at the company. We also asked them to share what they wanted the future communications in the company to be and how would the company look in 10 years as a result.

The interviews were followed by group discussions to identify the dream, design the future and agree the next steps, which included the criteria to help the implementation of the new communication process. The criteria 'for flawless, effective and connected communication', they agreed, would be adopted by each individual as a personal commitment to the team. The team decided to progress with the following three areas:

1 Each individual made personal commitment to the team. The commitments were: to find common ground with others; to focus communications on the business first and then on casual matters; to respect others and refrain from gossiping; to be flexible; to try to understand the other person's situation; to stay positive and to rely on each other for support; and finally to have fun.

2 The team agreed to use a board as a visual aid for communications between shifts. The board would reside at the supervisor's desk and serve as a visual management tool to communicate the status of the production line between shift changes. It would also bring visibility to any issues and allow other

avenues of communication between shifts. Initially the board was to be updated by supervisors and audited by the lead supervisor.

3 Finally, the team agreed to put in place a mentoring programme to help existing staff with anything they might need help for in the operations. The mentoring programme was initially meant for operators and supervisors only, but it was agreed that it could grow from there.

The idea of having a board as a visual aid for communication had already come up on the first day, while the other two items were direct outcomes of the Appreciative Inquiry process on the second day. Unlike at the end of the first day, the end of the second day found the team energized and excited about the new communications process.

The plant manager told me that he had felt the event was shaky after the first day, but that at the end of the second day it really had come together very well. He was 'extremely pleased with the results'.

The team was so excited about starting their action items that they ended up implementing all of the tasks on the action plan ahead of schedule. We monitored the state of the process for three months and saw many benefits for the company: shifts started faster with the new process; the required information was communicated properly; and errors in communication causing line down-time went down from about one a day to zero during the first three months of monitoring. In addition, self-reported morale was higher and the level was sustained over the period of at least three months.

Reflections

My own take-away for this experience was in realizing that the team really needed two approaches to be successful. They needed the technical tools that a traditional problem-solving approach brought, and they needed a way to address the more complex and ambiguous issue underlining good communications. I don't believe that in this specific case the event would have been successful without both. Even though many good ideas had already been identified on the first day, there was no real desire to make changes at that stage. The project didn't seem to address many of the team's concerns, so they probably wouldn't have carried it forward effectively if the communications concerns had not been addressed in a positive way (trying to solve the interpersonal relational issues with a problem-solving approach would not have helped as much). In addition, some of the ideas that were identified from the Appreciative Inquiry would not have been identified otherwise, and they complemented the technical solutions well. Above all, the Appreciative Inquiry helped release energy and establish the commitment to the change.

Ankit is a Lean Six Sigma consultant based in Atlanta, Georgia. He has an industrial engineering undergraduate degree from Georgia Institute of Technology and a Masters degree in positive organizational development from Case Western Reserve University in Cleveland, Ohio. He has worked with Dell Computers as a Lean consultant, where he was introduced to Lean Six Sigma. In his consulting, he combines traditional problem-solving with tools from positive psychology to enable success in each situation. He can be contacted through e-mail: ankit@theleanwayconsulting.com.

Our fourth story, by David Hansen, explores the application of Strength-based Lean Six Sigma as a successful approach to daily operations tasks at one of Novo Nordisk's production plants. This is particularly useful as much of the work we do with Lean Six Sigma is done day-to-day and outside the framework of a formal Kaizen or improvement event. David has picked three common operational challenges, and in the following story he shows us how they are handled successfully with a strength-based approach. His findings build on the success story from Henrik Kongsbak.

CASE STUDY   Strength-based Lean as a leadership approach – by David Hansen

Imagine if my employees did what I told them to do. That would be the worst thing that could happen! Bo, Production Director, Novo Nordisk (a medium-sized Danish manufacturing facility)

Having visited many organizations that work with continuous improvement, I have seen distinctively different versions of Lean leadership implemented. Sometimes the task of creating long-term employee commitment to continuous improvement is shadowed by focusing on short-term goals. In other places, I was struck by a clearly energized dedication towards long-term commitment where everyone took responsibility for 'striding for excellence'.

From 2011 until 2013 I followed and researched the daily management practices at Novo Nordisk, a medium-sized Danish manufacturing facility exhibiting such energized dedication. As the introductory quote from their production director shows, management clearly believes in initiative and in engaging the strengths of their employees. At the same time, they are committed to Lean manufacturing throughout all of their operations. They use their unique strength-based approach to Lean Six Sigma to handle daily challenges in operations management. By focusing on strengths, establishing a generative environment, and using affirmative future images together with Lean manufacturing philosophy they have taken a significant step towards building sustainable excellence in their operations. The following stories highlight some of their best applications and the outcomes they were able to generate.

Challenge 1: Engaging people's best strengths at work

Do some people have a repertoire of strengths that they just don't bring to work? Could engaging these strengths lead to unexpected but crucial success?

One morning I met with three machine operators from the company. They told me, 'Years ago, we decided we wanted to retire in this company – that meant we needed to take more responsibility – we needed to help the company stay competitive and significantly increase its productivity.' They knew some ideas had to come directly from the knowledge at shop-floor level. The managers wouldn't be able to achieve this on their own.

That day, the machine operators were on their way to present their daring ideas for crucial changes to a scheduling system in front of 30 managers. They proposed a significant operational change that would affect the entire planning system for scheduling how many machine operators had to work and when. For years, management had focused on small efficiency improvements but largely ignored the potential in questioning the scheduling of operators' working hours. The operators' idea would allow the factory to operate with 20 per cent less people provided they would accept a more flexible schedule. In their view this was a crucial improvement in order to keep the facility competitive: 'We need to be cheaper than our American sister facility. I want to show how competitive we can be as a production plant in Denmark so that perhaps more production is transferred here.' The other operator continued, 'Obviously, it is not popular to say that we have too many operators. We may lose jobs. Some may say that we will eliminate 20 per cent of the jobs but we would argue that we will save 80 per cent of them and it is necessary in order to help the factory survive.' Their Kaizen contributions were clearly not limited to just small daily operational improvements but also focused on changing the larger systems.

We arrived at the conference room. The 30 managers were ready and curious. The three guys were getting nervous. One told me, 'I really don't like presenting. If I could just do my job I would prefer that. But I want to do this to help us survive.'

After the presentation, the managers were impressed by the new ideas and by the shop floor employees' dedication. Some were sceptical, 'Great idea, but what would the union say?'... 'Can it work in practice?'... 'It'll be too hard to implement!'

We left the room and the operators calmed down... 'Do you think they want to try it?' 'I don't know... I think they got an alternative view, and that is good.'

Six months later, the struggle to improve the system bore fruit. The planning system was first tested in one part of (and later in the entire) facility. It required extensive negotiations with the union, but in the end it led to both savings and also better working conditions, according to the remaining operators, as they now had better options for improving the work processes.

This story exemplifies how some people have unexpected strengths that aren't often used at work. Why did these shop floor workers get engaged in large-scale improvements that went beyond their defined job responsibilities? What motivated them? Their answers to these questions were intriguing:

> I just want to do my job and whatever I can to contribute... But I don't want to be a manager.

> I like to see that I have been a part of creating something.

> I like working with different people. I want to be part of the best team or the best factory. I like to be part of something bigger.

They all wanted to contribute to the bigger picture. They didn't want to just do what they were told: they wanted to use their brains at work.

One of the most important challenges for managers of daily operations in any organization is how to bring the strengths of everyone into the game. Jack Welch was asked about the most important leadership challenge for the 21st century and his answer was simple: 'To bring every mind into the game!' Only when we engage everyone's strengths can a true improvement culture be sustained: when machine operators see the need to change the larger systems and get engaged with it rather than expect management to solve it.

One of the operators summarized the most important foundation for their engagement: 'When we accepted that the managers were the best at leading and organizing the work... And when they accepted that we were the best at operating the machines... When we accepted each other's strengths, we were able to shift the situation.'

As a contrast, in another company, I met a technician who always did a good professional job but rarely anything beyond what was expected of him. One day his manager heard that he was running for mayor in the local city, and that he was really good at mobilizing people for a higher cause. The manager realized that this strength had never showed up at work; it was hidden in his private life. This is an example for the huge potential that often remains unrealized because personal strengths have not been identified and activated at work.

To conclude the story, the core of taking a strength-based approach to Lean leadership is in finding ways to access and build on people's most useful strengths – even the unexpected ones. As Marcus Buckingham puts it: *Average managers play checkers, while great managers play chess*. They see that every piece is different, with different strengths, and use this tactically. There is a huge hidden potential in doing so. What can you do to engage more of your colleagues' strengths at work?

Challenge 2: Engaging everyone in improvements

Who should be engaged in improvements in order to have an improvement culture? Can we really get everyone engaged? Who are the best experts with the best solutions? How can we access their knowledge? How can we engage everyone's knowledge to strengthen the improvement culture? These questions often come up during continuous improvement initiatives that hope to establish an improvement culture. Often, the technical systems for creating improvements get implemented (such as idea banks and improvement meetings) but after a while people are no longer engaged in improvements. A true improvement culture is missing, a culture where the status quo can be regularly challenged, safely.

In the following example, the production management team handled a strategic change in the factory by accessing and engaging the collective knowledge of the whole system to find the best solution for a significant and pressing operational challenge.

One morning, the production director received a new production forecast that was substantially different from the one the plant was currently following. A former product had to be insourced back to the factory and produced in parallel with the existing, newer product. Since the entire factory had been optimized for one product, this posed complex challenges. The team leaders and production manager held a meeting to agree on how to handle the change. A project manager had already been assigned at the corporate level to help handle the process, and several internal Lean consultants were also available. So, how should they proceed with the change?

During the meeting, the production director and the team leaders decided they wanted to kick off with a focus on two things:

1 establishing a shared affirmative future image for the change;

2 engaging everyone, not just the experts, in identifying and creating the necessary improvements.

They planned to start with a one-day summit, having the entire production department in the room in order to engage everyone's strengths in getting the best out of the new situation. Some think that it's expensive or impossible to close down production for a day, but the production director argued that 'every successful sports team takes time out when they need sudden changes, and it's always worth it'.

The day started with the production director talking about the new situation. He framed his presentation carefully in order to highlight future possibilities in the situation and thereby allow for ideas to emerge, rather than making everyone nervous about the future and thus adopting a defensive posture, which could have been the case with a 'burning platform' story. Instead, he highlighted the opportunity to show their ability to create improvements and therefore position the plant well in the global competition for the next product launch. After some time discussing the future image, the participants agreed to this overall direction.

The next phase was to identify each of the teams' strengths and assess which strengths would be most useful in achieving success. It was carried out in three steps (see Figure 17.2):

1 using paired interviews where everyone was asked to identify the strengths of the team through sharing an experience of peak performance;

2 sharing the best stories with everyone to get inspired;

3 selecting the three most important team strengths for the entire department to hear.

Observing this process, I could see how connections between people were established when they interviewed each other, and how they became more energized. It was even more interesting when the teams had to select and agree on three strengths. One team of technicians started with a somewhat sceptical attitude; most sat with their arms crossed. Gradually, as the task progressed, the atmosphere changed. It was great to see these competitive guys trying to convince the others that one particular strength would be more useful than another. Not only did they end up with a list of three strengths to present to the rest of the department, they had also convinced themselves they actually had the necessary resources to succeed with the challenge. This phase culminated in plenary presentations where all teams shared the strengths they wanted to use to achieve success.

The final phase focused on collecting ideas and knowledge from all teams on how to realize the affirmative future image. They were asked three guiding questions:

1 What are the necessary improvements in order to achieve success?

2 What do we already know we want to do as a team?

3 What improvements require support from others in order to be able to realize them?

FIGURE 17.2 The three steps taken to identify the team's most important strengths

Note the distinction between asking for input to solve a future problem versus identifying what should be done to achieve an affirmative future image. Since the change in this case focused on insourcing a product – a task that many of the participants had successful past experiences with – the question allowed for both a critical perspective of what needed to be done and a more generative perspective of what could be done to exceed the expectations and past achievements. The teams' process facilitators were aware of this distinction and made sure both perspectives were considered in the discussions. After an hour the teams presented their ideas and all had a chance to comment and applaud the presentations. The inputs were collected and passed on to the new project manager, but each of the teams took responsibility for their own three suggestions. During lunch some of the ideas were already moving forward. At the end of this four-hour off-site session, no one had their arms crossed: most people were standing around the whiteboard engaged in lively discussions.

So, what were the outcomes? Twenty-two executable ideas were fed to the project manager, and 24 actions were adopted by the team. The most important improvements that started during the day were a new idea for in-process quality control and an idea on how to increase flexibility and support between the different teams when cross-functional effort was needed.

The indirect outcomes may have been even more important for the success of the change. One of the participants mentioned in an online evaluation that 'it is important that everyone feels they are a part of the decisions that are made. It's great we've been asked because now it is much easier to implement the changes.' What a great testament to the high level of engagement achieved by taking this approach!

Having everybody in the room at the same time also gives opportunities for quick changes because decision makers are available. Common excuses for inaction (eg management or other teams will not allow an idea) can be instantly tested to allow the idea to develop instead of being eliminated without reason.

FIGURE 17.3 The three steps taken to generate input about improvements necessary to achieve success

A change activity like this is strength-based for two reasons. First, it focuses on getting all the strengths in the entire department engaged by involving everyone. Second, its focus is on realizing an affirmative future image, instead of trying to avoid the effects of a problematic external force. Positive future images have two purposes: to elevate the strengths in the organization by aligning efforts and creating a shared sense of confidence; and to enable a change of thinking paradigm and the emergence of optional solutions.

The production director made three points at the start of the day:

1 Our shared input is important for success.

2 Our subsequent engagement is crucial.

3 We need to identify and mobilize our strengths.

This belief in the power of getting everyone involved from the start and establishing a clear, shared image of the desired future helps make it meaningful to everyone in the factory and empowers them to execute improvements. What an excellent way to cultivate an improvement culture!

Challenge 3: Managing daily improvement activities from a strength-based perspective

What about daily improvements? Should Strength-based Lean Six Sigma focus on solving problems or on identifying and elevating success?

Finding the answer to this question had been a puzzle for the managers in the production facility for some time. The facility had a well-developed performance measurement system in place and therefore data about efficiency levels was available on a daily basis. This can lead to quick identification of problems and a focus on solving them.

But was this actually an issue in this case? According to the production director, it was. They needed to actively work with this habit, because as he said, 'When the core of our work processes lies in technical problem solving, it is easy to fall back to a deficit-focused mindset that does not foster effective collaboration.' He concluded that while problem solving is a necessary part of the everyday management at an effective production facility, it is also necessary to actively find ways to balance the problem focus with a more engaging mindset in order to sustain the desired collaborative improvement culture.

Management at the facility realized that this had to be integrated with everyday actions in order to influence the culture. They therefore implemented three strength-based practices:

1. **Learning from and reinforcing positive deviances in performance.** This is carried out systematically and handled just as if it were a problem to solve. Following a template with specially crafted questions designed to identify the root causes for the success, people get assigned to the task of understanding, learning from and reinforcing a positive performance deviance, such as a record high efficiency for a week or an example of a successful project carried out in a team. Although this practice may seem simple, it can be challenging to isolate root causes for success, and often the answers given are generic and high-level factors such as good planning, coordination and professional work. However, surprising findings sometimes come out of the analysis, and even trivial responses such as 'good planning' can be an occasion to reinforce practices that might otherwise be forgotten. As one internal Lean consultant explained, 'I had tried to tell the team for months that they should spend a longer time in the planning phase before they went into doing. They never took my advice seriously. Now, after exploring their recent great validation, they concluded that the validations were effective because of good planning. Now they finally got it!' Another advantage about learning from positive deviances is that it usually leads to a focus on the entire work system rather than small technical issues that are taken out of context. It is necessary to build up a systems perspective to really create a sustainable improvement culture.

2. **Strength-based process confirmation.** The team leaders spend a substantial amount of time at the shop floor where they ensure team members follow the work standards. They had been looking for gaps between standard and observed actions in order to correct them. Now they have changed their perspectives; they enter the shop floor with the assumption that team members are likely to have a good reason when they choose to take a different action. Often they end up improving the work process from the latest standard based on their individual strengths. This has led to very different conversations between team leaders and operators. Because team leaders actively look for positive actions, they create more constructive conversations that result in ideas for updates to the standard work procedures. Most importantly, though, is the change in atmosphere – the employees testify that they feel more involved – this of course reinforces the

desired culture and findings can be surprising. For example, they realized that one of the operators could manage the production halls while the other three were at lunch. When asked how he could manage the work of four people, he shared many good practices he had never shared before. This shows the power of active leadership by asking 'different questions'.

3. A positive work environment with more fun. The final practice that enables improvement activities to be driven from a strength-based approach is a serious approach to creating a positive work environment with more fun. This continuous task is referred to as 'funny business'. Almost every month, as well as spontaneously, an event is carried out simply for the purpose of creating a fun and positive environment at work. These events generate positive emotions and energy to feed on. For example, a group of samba dancers touring the facility; big 'Where's Waldo' cardboard figures with inspiring questions hidden around the factory; and funny videos shared at serious presentations. The value of creating fun and positive emotions at work has been well described in Barbara Fredrickson's research on positive emotions. Incorporating these large 'funny business' events as well as small daily practices to generate positive emotions are other ways of reinforcing a creative and strength-focused improvement culture as part of daily management.

So what are the key themes I can see that work particularly well to enable a strength-based approach to Lean leadership?

The three challenges I described show strength-based practices to daily Lean leadership. They share four principles that could form the basis for future operations management:

1 **Engage people's best strengths at work.** When everyone brings their best selves and their strengths to work, and when the work is adjusted to fit different preferences, better alignment and therefore high performance can be achieved.

2 **Create shared affirmative images of the future as a basis for improvements.** Affirmative images of the future can create a shared sense of meaning that encourages everyone to see possibilities and empowers them to create improvements.

3 **Learn from and reinforce positive deviances.** When management practices require problem-solving *and* learning from as well as reinforcing positive deviances on a daily basis, a more innovative improvement culture is established; one that not only focuses on simple technical issues but the whole work system.

4 **Actively create and enhance positive emotions at work.** When a work system builds its culture based on generating positive relations, emotions and energy, it creates a safe environment for people. Creativity, initiative and passion can then thrive.

David Hansen is an industrial PhD candidate at the technical university of Denmark. He is affiliated with the division of Production and Service Management and the company Resonans. He carries out action research focused on how to create employee-driven improvement cultures based on Lean and Strength-based approaches to change. He can be contacted through e-mail: dh@resonans.dk.

Summary

The case stories in this chapter share common themes of success in applying a strength-based approach to Lean Six Sigma process improvement and daily leadership. They are:

1 Start business improvement journeys by reframing a problem or a need to a *shared* opportunity or aspiration that holds a deep meaning for the organization and can drive everyone towards it rather than away from it.

2 Engage the whole system and its wealth of strengths, knowledge, past experience and expertise – those that were acquired at work as well as those that are more evident outside of work. Another advantage with this approach is the quick resolution in a collaborative way of potential concerns or objections.

3 The use of 'different questions' – questions that focus on what is wanted rather than what isn't, what works well rather than what doesn't and what is already known rather than what isn't.

4 Adopt an inquisitive mindset – a mindset which holds that no single person, however senior or experienced, knows all the solutions. It also includes allowing ourselves to be surprised by ideas and solutions regardless of where they came from, rather than judging or evaluating them straight away. The best solutions emerge through dialogue and explorations of topics that matter to the people in the organization.

5 The importance of developing strong connections and relationships. These are significantly strengthened when we learn what each person's strengths are and what they are capable of.

6 Use stories alongside quantitative data. Stories of past experiences and future aspirations are a very powerful source of knowledge.

In the next chapter I will switch the focus from 'Delivery' to 'Destiny'. The chapter describes what else could be possible in future for Strength-based Lean Six Sigma. In other words, what will take this topic even further than where I have taken it so far?

Before moving to the next chapter, here are a few questions for you to consider:

1 How has your understanding of Strength-based Lean Six Sigma been further enhanced through these stories?

2 Which ideas from the case stories did you find most exciting and relevant to your work? Which are most compelling for you to try?

3 How can you integrate the themes of success I describe in the summary with your work?

Destiny – opening the door to the future of Strength-based Lean Six Sigma

This book has primarily focused on integrating the thinking, techniques, tools and principles of 'classic' Lean Six Sigma (the 'first generation'), with the tools, principles and philosophy behind strength-based change. This combination leads us to Strength-based Lean Six Sigma (the 'second generation').

In this final chapter of the book, I would like to explore the destiny of the second generation. What *are* the possibilities for Strength-based Lean Six Sigma? I would also like to open the door for another promising development – a deeper integration of strength-focus and process improvement including positive psychology and emotional intelligence. This will undoubtedly deliver a third, possibly even more powerful, generation. Table 18.1 summarizes the progress between generations.

The full spectrum of possibilities for the second generation

Imagining the future possibilities for Strength-based Lean Six Sigma truly inspires me. I can see continued expansion both in the breadth of

TABLE 18.1 The different generations of Lean Six Sigma

	Ways to practise
First generation Lean Six Sigma	Identify and eliminate waste, defects and bottlenecks to deliver more value to the customers efficiently and consistently.
Second generation Lean Six Sigma	Reframe the first generation by focusing on what is wanted: identifying where value, perfection and flow already exist and using them to deliver more value and efficiency.
Third generation Lean Six Sigma	In addition to the ideas from the second generation, this generation fully integrates the full spectrum of existing personal strengths, passions, values, purposes, personal 'flow' (as defined by Positive Psychology) and emotional intelligence.

A few words about the personal state of 'flow'

The concept of 'flow' was first introduced by Mihály Csíkszentmihályi (1990). Flow is a mental state in which a person performing an activity is fully immersed in a feeling of energized focus, full involvement and enjoyment in their activity. Flow is characterized by complete absorption in what one is doing.

According to Csíkszentmihályi, flow is driven by completely focused motivation. It is a single-minded immersion and represents perhaps the ultimate experience in harnessing the emotions in the service of performing and learning. In this state of flow, emotions are positive, energized, and the individual experiences a feeling of spontaneous joy while performing a task. Flow can also be defined as a state of deep focus on nothing but the activity.

applications and experiences, the depth of knowledge and the reach of this practice. Like all strength-based approaches to change, this practice helps release human creativity, engagement and energy which are all key enablers of such growth. Here are the key opportunities ahead:

1 **The opportunity to expand the practice.** As the practice of Strength-based Lean Six Sigma is still nascent, my first hope for it is to see it expanding around the world much in the same way as Lean Thinking and Six Sigma did. I also hope it will happen more quickly. The energy and creativity it releases, the engagement it creates and the impact many feel when they experience it, not to mention the final results, all of these will drive the growth of the practice and its expansion so that it touches businesses of different sizes and sectors as well as public services around the world.

2 **The opportunity to engage with people in organizations quickly, more positively and in a sustainable way.** If we want to get the people who work in organizations to drive efficiency on an ongoing basis, they have to *want* to do it. This cannot be driven sustainably through reward mechanisms. I believe that if we help people see the value they regularly contribute to their organization, its processes and the end customer, the engagement will be easier and longer lasting than when we focus on wastes and defects. It is also intrinsically motivating and therefore a stronger driver.

3 **The opportunity to reach engaging continuous learning, thus ensuring sustainable efficiency programmes.** By training people at all levels inside organizations in some simple Solution Focus, Positive Deviance and Appreciative Inquiry concepts and tools that are relevant to the areas they are in charge of and the people they interact with, we are more likely to enable ongoing discovery of what works and co-creation of what will work even better. This, to me, is a very energizing and effective way to achieve continuous improvement.

4 **The opportunity to truly affect the whole system.** Appreciative Inquiry is, by definition, a whole-system change approach. Lean Thinking was always meant to be one, yet few organizations can claim to have implemented it at that level. For those who have implemented Lean on a whole-system level, the journey to get there has likely been long and

challenging. For the first time ever, there is a clear opportunity to truly apply Lean Six Sigma at the whole-organization level that has eluded us for so many years by using a strength-based approach. In fact, it can reach even further and include whole systems (ie the vital connections with suppliers, customers and even regulators). Strength-based Lean Six Sigma has the power to motivate the whole system and its stakeholders. This means a much higher probability of implementing the change we wish to drive and a lower risk arising from disconnects with key stakeholders.

5 **Working on process improvement *together with* organizational change – not just one or the other.** Strength-based Lean Six Sigma offers the opportunity to drive organizational change together with process improvement, rather than focusing on one or the other. Currently many organizations find themselves driving either a cultural change programme or an efficiency programme. In the worst cases, they are driving two or even more programmes (of change and of efficiency), but the programmes are disconnected and either run in parallel or drive the organization in conflicting directions. While Lean practitioners often advocate the need for a culture shift to support the efficiency drive, the approach taken can be mechanistic and based on levers of control through standards, documentation, rewards and skills training programmes. In my view, Strength-based Lean taps into the softer (some prefer to call it the 'human') side of change while still focusing on delivering more value.

Of course, there may be many other opportunities and possibilities for the practice of Strength-based Lean Six Sigma and you may have your own hopes and visions that will direct you in your learning and practice.

My work to date has been centred primarily on the transition to the second generation – the integration of strength-based approaches to organizational change with Lean Six Sigma. In parallel, Jeremy Scrivens, another thought leader in the area of Strength-based Lean Six Sigma and a colleague, has been exploring and developing the thinking behind a practice that may become the third generation. He believes (as do I) that the future will lead to a full integration of personal flow, individual strengths and emotional intelligence with the second generation of Strength-based Lean Six Sigma. In this final part of both this chapter and the book, we will go beyond the current possibilities I have identified so far to look at a vision for the future based on Jeremy Scrivens' thoughts today.

The case for the third generation

Much of the focus of the first generation of Six Sigma and Lean Process and business improvement has been on eradicating waste and reducing errors by 'making value flow'. The focus has been on making the customer process flow by looking for what isn't working, is failing or is broken, then identifying the root causes of the problems and applying the fix. The conversations around this work have invariably been around the 'what' and 'how' of our work, not the 'why'. As a consequence, we have failed to engage people, to get them to buy into the changes with passion. Many do not 'flow' with the changes to their work processes and methods made as a result of these projects.

The pursuit of waste and error eradication in customer and business processes is a noble intention but has fallen short of its potential benefits because the focus of much of this activity is on problems not possibilities; on *muda* (Japanese for 'waste'), not meaning; on controls, not creativity.

Focusing on what is broken or not working (eg the seven types of waste) and looking to 'close the gap' between the ideal state as defined in the existing business standard (eg Six Sigma quality) becomes the centre of activity. The focus is actually on the tasks we execute. Rarely, if ever, do we – the change and improvement agents or consultants – invite people on the shop floor to engage in conversations around 'why we are in business' or 'who we are as a community'; it has always been about fixing problems or errors in business processes.

When you engage people in the 'why' questions of business, you go into the very heart of the meaningful issues of work and life, and how they interact and influence each other:

1 Why do I (we) exist?

2 Who are we being?

3 Why am I (are we) in this business?

4 What are our deeply held values?

5 What are we really good at?

6 What is our destiny or purpose?

7 What is the difference we are making to our world, and what legacy will we leave behind?

Perhaps the most brilliant author on the Toyota Production Systems is Kiyoshi Suzaki who wrote extensively on the techniques of eradicating waste in Japanese factories in his superb book *The New Shop Floor Management* (1993). This was all about the 'what' and 'how' of our work.

In 2002, Suzaki wrote another book, called *Results from the Heart*, in which he progressed in his thinking to the point where he said that in order for people to be fully effective they need to be engaged from the heart around values, care, vision and meaning in their work. He saw every person as president of their own company, not just as an operator of processes.

This means that people partner with each other as co-creators around the 'what' we do and 'how' we do it, but more importantly around the 'why' we exist. This is much more holistic because it engages the whole person in their work: hands (skills), head (rational thinking) and heart (connecting who we are to a deeper, meaningful purpose).

This is where the notion of discovering and building on our core strengths through strength-based change led to a transformation in my thinking around what the true and noble purposes of Six Sigma and Lean Thinking were really about: *making people flow*, an extension of the idea of making processes flow.

For example, if I apply the disciplines of Appreciative Inquiry to look at first generation Six Sigma and Lean and ask, 'What is the best of these disciplines to take forward into the future?', I would say that it is the idea of flow. If I were to ask the question, 'What could the future of Six Sigma and Lean look like by building on its best contribution to date; what could they become?', I would answer with the following vision or 'possibility statement':

> The future will see the focus switch from mapping the 'as is' and the 'to be' of *process* flow to mapping the 'as is' of *people* flow, with the goal of creating positive organizations where everyone is fully contributing in their work because they are engaged with their hands, their head and their heart. We will see the focus shift from reducing variation in processes to the increasing variation of people's talents. These are the talents that will be discovered and engaged in creative conversations where the future is not yet known, but the possibilities and benefits are endless. This can finally lead us to the positive version of Six Sigma quality.

The first generation of Six Sigma and Lean Thinking have focused on the intellectual pursuit of quality and efficiency through waste and defect elimination. The application of strength-based approaches to Lean Six Sigma helps us flip the coin to pursue value and efficiency using the best of the past and present. It also opens the door to much more!

Simon Sinek says that every organization knows *what* it does, some know *how* they do it, but few know *why* they do it. 'Why' means clarity around who we really are and what we truly believe.

The next generation of Lean Six Sigma will engage the heart in a search for what it takes to experience meaningful flow – a quest that is as much spiritual and emotional as it is rational. That is why Appreciative Inquiry has been so liberating for this conversation: it engages people around stories that they care about, stories that are meaningful to them and therefore are deeply engaging. If you start with this approach, you will engage them around using the statistics and tools of rational business and process improvement – these will become the 'servants of the heart, not the masters'.

Why does it matter? It matters because Gallup research points out that only 30 per cent of the workforce in the United States, 18 per cent in Australia and 16 per cent in the UK are engaged at work. This implies that only a small minority of the Western workforce is engaged or fully contributing at work! True engagement starts from the heart, then the head and finally the hands. When all three are engaged, people flow in their work. The one in five who *are* engaged, are engaged from who they are: their natural wiring or talents; their beliefs; what motivates them. In other words, they are engaged intrinsically in business change. Engaged people voluntarily contribute all of who they are to their work, colleagues, customers and community, thus creating endless possibilities!

Third generation Lean Six Sigma Projects that start by engaging people around 'why' – uncovering strengths, values, talents and what we believe as individuals and as communities – will be more successful than the first generation projects, which tried to engage people solely from 'what' and 'how'. They will help us move from technical change to adaptive change, from rational thinking and conversations (head) to emotional growth, which comes from the heart or self or spirit; that is, it is intrinsic. Individuals have intrinsic spirit, and so do teams, organizations and communities. The following story from Jeremy Scrivens' work with a local government organization shows what could be possible.

CASE STUDY   Big River Shire: applying the next generation of Strength-based Lean Six Sigma – a case story

The Environmental Health (EH) Team at Big River Shire was in crisis. Simon, their executive manager, decided to intervene, as he explained:

> This team was extremely busy and was having trouble coping emotionally. Not only was the leader the coordinator of EH, he was also Municipal Recovery Manager, and required to respond to emergencies or community issues that could be constituted as a disaster. In 2009 the team had been dealing with three major environmental crises. They felt a deep sense of despair with the workload. Team members got emotional when discussing work. I wanted to help them get back to a resonant team, while still managing the priorities – and I didn't want to lose good people in the process. I wanted to help them manage the busy workload long-term, including coming up with some innovative solutions.

The demand for health services was increasing within the Big River Shire community because the population was growing rapidly, but resources were tight. Within the health team, morale was falling, service standards and time frames slipping. In-trays were piling up with uncompleted septic tank planning permits. This was a period of sustained high stress, which exposed issues with the way the work got done, team values and communication. In the past the team had won a high reputation for the quality of its work with customers. Team members were highly respected by their peers and the community, but that reputation was at risk.

The team was under additional pressures: the shire had invested heavily in bringing in a Lean framework and announced a vision that saw higher levels of customer service being provided by shire service teams, including faster planning permit turnarounds. The team worked under a rigorous compliance regime that required ever-increasing attention being devoted to avoiding errors and ensuring adherence to external standards.

Fortunately, Simon saw this crisis as an opportunity for adaptive change, not as a problem to be fixed, even though the problem was big. His focus on innovative solutions was a key leadership trigger for the health team to approach the situation with a different mindset. Simon and the team recognized that the word 'crisis' came from a root word meaning 'a turning point, a decisive moment'. So, rather than focusing on fixing problems and returning to the status quo, the team switched to looking at the situation as an opportunity to build something new by taking the best of the past forward: the best for customers and the best for team members. They looked for what was good and how to amplify and extend it.

The team chose a key service process, the issuing of permits to install septic tanks. They mapped the 'as is' process *when it worked* to engage team members and customers rationally *and* emotionally.

Through facilitated Appreciative Inquiry conversations, the health team challenged the assumptions behind the way the work was being done, including the unspoken norms around the process. For example, focusing on what worked in the process provided the team with the confidence and trust to challenge issues that were considered taboo, such as why the current process had three inspection points that treated the plumbers as incompetent and untrustworthy and slowed the whole process down. The 'unspoken norm' turned out to be that the council was more afraid of the consequences of getting the process wrong one time out of a hundred, rather than right 99 times, so everything had slowed down. Many process-improvement conversations never challenge the unspoken norms, which go to deeply held beliefs and cultural norms: 'This is the way we do things around here – don't you dare ask why!'

The plumbers, as customers, were asked to identify the heroes in the health team. All organizations have heroes who appear in the company's myths and stories. These heroes symbolize the organization's strengths or Positive Core – the organization at its best. Heroes can be living legends in an organization's history. They are people we deeply admire and aspire to be like.

In this case, the 'living legend' for the plumbers was one health team member, Mary. She treated the plumbers as adults. She by-passed the compliance process by spending time with the plumbers on-site and getting agreement with them about each septic tank application. She did this because she was naturally talented or wired around seeing the world through relationships. When the plumbers lodged their applications with Mary, they went through the current process five times faster than applications lodged with health team members who didn't go out on-site and build relationships with them.

The focus on appreciating the process at its best released the team to look at everything: nothing was sacred or untouchable, including the shire's core values, structure, job designs, information technology, buildings, regulatory practices, myths, mindsets and symbols. For example, the team abolished the job title Community Compliance Officer because, at its best, the Septics Permit process was about front-end education and supporting the plumbers to self-regulate, not enforcing compliance. Adaptive change requires a broader lens than simply looking at work flows in isolation from the core values and beliefs about the way the world is.

Of course, problems with the process came to the surface. However, in the Appreciative Inquiry conversations, the team focused its energies on identifying the Septics Permit Service at its rational and emotional best for people (including people and process strengths), and then asking 'How can we create new ways of releasing and aligning more of these strengths, so that the weaknesses become irrelevant?'

Over the years, the health team had geared up their service processes to engage each other and their customers almost exclusively on a rational basis. A mindset of 'low trust' developed around avoiding errors and 'gap analysis', with a strong focus on achieving compliance. As a consequence, they had tended to model their business processes around a 'system equalizers', low risk, one-size-fits-all service. There were multiple checkpoints, low innovation and personal relationships and (mostly negative) feedback on a service performance designed to fix problems rather than release hope, innovation and meaning.

Using Appreciative Inquiry, the health team created 'possibility propositions' around a future where the current focus on compliance and reactive back-end checking of septic tank installations adapted to a more proactive front-end community education and well-being partnership process with plumbers.

Responsibility for the quality of the septics installation is now with the plumbers by their choice. The process has been rewired and assumes the plumbers and other applicants will do the right thing, with front-end education and positive feedback from the health officers supporting them. The new focus on self-regulation eliminates the need for time-consuming inspections by health officers before a Permit to Use is issued.

Next, the health team decided to identify and integrate their unique talents using the 'business DNA natural talents profiling system'. They wanted to find the core personal behaviours and attitudes most likely to engage customers rationally and emotionally in the next stage of the 'to be' process and build these into future recruitment and performance review processes for new team members. They also learned to identify the different needs of their customers and adapt their behaviour to meet individual needs.

The health team identified substantial benefits and payoffs to all stakeholders, including rational engagers such as cost savings, improved service quality, reduction of backlogs and customer queues, shorter service timelines and freeing up extra capacity in the shire to 'do more with less'.

In addition, the team identified significant emotional benefits and payoffs, including a new way of working together that reduced the boring and repetitive aspects of the work, decreased stress in staff members, released hope and innovation around doing things better, increased energy and commitment to a shared future and set up for growth.

Health Team Leader John added:

We have eliminated much of the stopping and starting. We always thought Septics was a good process when we started. If we had mapped it looking at it just as a process, we would not have made the changes we had. The backlogs have gone. It was the stories from the plumbers that made the difference. Listening to their positive stories, and feeling special and then listening to their ideas for improvements. Also feeling empowered to question anything in and around the current process.

Six months ago it would have taken closer to 10 days for most people to get their permits. With the new process it will be closer to five days without hassles because the service will flow. The five days represents what the customer wants and we have redesigned the process to achieve this. We will do this without increasing staff numbers and also free up more time to do other interesting work. We will still be compliant but will contribute more. We all feel less stress and have the time to work with our customers on creating new ways of providing a better service.

Executive Manager Simon couldn't hide his delight:

I found the Appreciative Inquiry process to be incredibly innovative and solution-oriented. The health team was in crisis through no fault of their own and Appreciative Inquiry helped bring them back to the efficient and customer-focused team that I knew before. They achieved amazing results in a short time. The team is now re-energized, has a clear vision, and is clearly empowered to bring about their own success in association with the enterprise's goals. It was the application of Appreciative Inquiry to engaging and integrating people's emotional needs that made the difference.

Summary

As you can see in this chapter, the potential destiny for Strength-based Lean Six Sigma is truly inspiring and full of possibilities for the practice of the second generation I have covered in this book, as well as additional future development through the third generation.

Globally, there is increasing interest in the application of strength-based change to Lean Six Sigma, and a growing number of innovative practitioners who combine a strength/positive approach to how they work with Lean Six Sigma. What is exciting to me is learning about the various ways they do it. There are simply endless possibilities – our creativity is unlimited and this journey can go far!

My dream is that Strength-based Lean Six Sigma is proven to enable a step-change in how we think of our processes, how we go about improving them and eventually how we look at and interact with the organizations we work with. I hope that we shift away from seeing organizations and the people within them as problems waiting to be solved, and towards a true sense of appreciation and inquiry that sees organizations, their processes and their people as opportunities that are waiting to be discovered and tapped into. This book is a first step in this vision and my invitation to you to get involved in this exciting opportunity!

APPENDIX A

A comparison of deficit- and strength-based problem solving

This table provides a comparison of the different stages of problem solving from a deficit point of view (which is common in the practice of Lean Thinking and Six Sigma) to the approach taken in strength-based thinking. This useful comparison was created by Jackie Kelm, a well-known Appreciative Inquiry practitioner and thought leader, who created a unique approach for Appreciative Innovation and Engagement. For more details about this approach, visit http://www.youtube.com/watch?v=UF2RV_C0XuE.

TABLE A.1 Comparison between deficit- and strength-based approaches to problem solving

	Deficit-based problem solving	Strength-based problem solving
Starting point	Problem.	Problem or identified opportunity.
Determine	What is not wanted?	What is wanted?
When is it most useful?	Solving problems with equipment or automated processes where predictability level is high.	Addressing complex and unpredictable problems that affect whole systems where cause-and-effect relationships cannot be identified easily and where solutions are likely to emerge through wider conversation and exploration.

(Continued)

TABLE A.1 (Continued)

'As is' situation analysis	Root causes of failure: Spotting weaknesses, problem areas, breakdowns, failures and defects. Identify negative deviance from the norm.	Root cause of success: strengths and best practices, breakthroughs and high points of performance. Positive deviance from the norm.
Key tools	Surveys, assessments, data analysis.	Interviews, reframing, great practices, stories and studies. Data analysis about what works.
People involved	Task force/project team.	Task force/core group/project team with input from larger system and stakeholders.
Analysis output	What went wrong? Why? Who/What to blame? A list of possible solutions based on what does NOT work currently, relevant best practices from elsewhere (ideas we assume might work in our case). (Sometimes) a defined 'to be' state.	What works? What enables it? Who and what is to be celebrated and learnt from? A list of possible solutions based on what does work in our case (including one-off's) along with a collective vision of the ideal/hoped-for future.
Side effects	Resistance	Those involved gain energy, confidence and motivation.
The change process	Action planning and implementation with a problem-focused approach: What actions are still open? What is blocking or slowing an implementation? Who has not done what they have committed to?	Action planning using a strength approach: celebrating success and completed actions; finding new, creative ways to bypass block; learning from the progress made; finding what enabled us to make progress.

Change leaders	Managers, task force, leaders.	Shared ownership among managers, task force, employees and inspired participants from the wider system.
End result	Fix the problem (hopefully) and return to the status quo.	Create new and innovative possibilities exceeding the original problem ('from good to great').
Emotional impact (These outcomes are more likely the more deficit or strength-based approach we practise throughout the problem-solving journey.)	Fear, mistrust, defensiveness, disengagement (active or passive).	Enthusiasm, engagement, trust, cooperation and ownership.

Table A.1 highlights the benefits of the strength-based approach over the deficit-based. In reality, they are both useful. I invite you to consider and use both approaches as appropriate to the situations you are facing.

APPENDIX B

Where to learn more about strength-based change

If you found the ideas I presented in this book useful and would like to learn more about Strength-based Lean Six Sigma or the various strength-based approaches to change I have discussed, here are a few suggested favourite books, websites and training providers:

Strength-based Lean Six Sigma

Online resources

Strength-based Lean Six Sigma blog: www.almond-insight.co/sblss/blog/ – in this blog I capture my most recent thoughts, ideas and ongoing experiences in this practice.

Strength-based Lean Six Sigma group on LinkedIn – this group is a discussion forum to explore related topics and post questions. The group can be found here: http://www.linkedin.com/groups?gid=2503162.

Appreciative Inquiry

There are many excellent resources on Appreciative Inquiry in general and on its varied applications to individual, team, organizational and community change.

Training workshops

Attending an experience-based workshop is by far the best way to learn the practice of Appreciative Inquiry and acquire an in-depth understanding of its guiding principles, so that you can later apply them in your own practice. There are many excellent providers. In Europe, the best workshops are run by the Lincoln Workshop Series (www.appreciative-inquiry.co.uk). In the United States, NTL (www.ntl.org) is a leading provider; and in Canada, Innovation Works (http://innovationworks.ca/) is another excellent provider. I am one of the Appreciative Inquiry trainers for Lincoln Workshop Series and for NTL.

Books

The following selection includes some of my favourite books on Appreciative Inquiry:

1 Magruder Watkins, Jane, Mohr, Bernard and Kelly, Ralph (2011) *Appreciative Inquiry: Change at the speed of imagination* (2nd edn), Pfeiffer, New York

2 Kelm, Jacqueline (2005) *Appreciative Living: The principles of Appreciative Inquiry in personal life*, Venet Publishers, Wake Forest, NC

3 Lewis, Sarah, Passmore, Jonathan and Cantore, Stefan (2011) *Appreciative Inquiry for Change Management: Using AI to facilitate organizational development* (2nd edn), Kogan Page, London

4 Cooperrider, David, Whitney, Diana and Stavros, Jacqueline (2008) *Appreciative Inquiry Handbook for Leaders of Change* (2nd edn), Crown Publishing, Brunswick, OH

5 Whitney, Diana and Trosten Bloom, Amanda (2010) *The Power of Appreciative Inquiry: A practical guide to positive change* (2nd edn), Berrett-Koehler, San Francisco, CA

6 Ludema, James, Whitney, Diana, Mohr, Bernard and Griffin, Thomas J (2003) *The Appreciative Inquiry Summit, a practitioner guide for leading large scale change*, Berrett-Koehler, San Francisco, CA

7 Hamond, Sue Annis (1996) *The Thin Book of Appreciative Inquiry* (2nd edn), Thin Book Publishing, Bend, OR

8 Stavros, Jacqueline and Hinrichs, Gina (2009) *The Thin Book of SOAR: Building strengths-based strategy*, Thin Book Publishing, Bend, OR

Online resources

In addition to these books, AI Practitioner (www.aipractitioner.com) is an invaluable online journal with excellent articles by leading thinkers, professionals and active practitioners in the field of Appreciative Inquiry.

The AI Commons (http://appreciativeinquiry.case.edu/) is a great online resource which is full of case stories and other useful materials.

The AI Listserv (http://mailman.business.utah.edu:8080/mailman/listinfo/ailist) is a lively discussion forum and a great learning resource.

The Begeistring Community (www.networkplace.eu) is the European network around Appreciative Inquiry and strength-based change. It organizes two events each year in which practitioners meet and learn from each other.

SOAR Strategy: www.soarstrategy.com

The Taos Institute: www.taosinstitute.net

Finally, there are many excellent Appreciative Inquiry groups on LinkedIn. One of my favourites is called Appreciative Inquiry 1st.

Solution Focus

Training workshops

Excellent Solution Focus Workshops are provided by SF WORK (www.sfwork.com). Their website has many free articles and other resources.

Books

1 Jackson, Paul and McKergow, Mark (2007) *The Solutions Focus: Making coaching and change SIMPLE* (2nd rev edn), Nicholas Brealey Publishing, London (this book is available in 11 languages)

2 McKergow, Mark and Clarke, Jenny (2007) *Solutions Focus Working: 80 real-life lessons for successful organizational change*, Solutions Books, Cheltenham, UK

3 Rohrig, Peter and Clarke, Jenny (eds) (2008) *57 SF Activities for Facilitators and Consultants: Putting Solutions Focus into action*, Solutions Books, Cheltenham, UK

4 Berg, Insoo Kim and Szabó, Peter (2005) *Brief Coaching for Lasting Solutions*, WW Norton, New York (companion DVD available)

5 Meier, Daniel (2005) *Team Coaching with the Solution Circle: A practical guide to Solution Focused team development*, Solutions Books, Cheltenham, UK

6 Fredrike Bannink (2010) 1001 Solution-Focused Questions: Handbook for Solution-Focused interviewing (2nd edn), WW Norton, New York

Online and other resources

SFCT, the Association for SF consultants and trainers: www.asfct. org. SFCT publishes *InterAction: the journal of Solution Focus in Organizations* (http://www.ingentaconnect.com/content/sfct/inter).

SOL World organizes conferences and other SF-related events for consultants and managers: www.solworld.org.

Positive Deviance

Although most of the current practice of Positive Deviance is centred on community development and the voluntary sector, I believe that the principles of Positive Deviance are equally useful within organizations. Here are my favourite resources on Positive Deviance.

Books

1 Pascale, Richard, Sternin, Jerry and Sternin, Monique (2010) *The Power of Positive Deviance: How unlikely innovators solve the world's toughest problems*, Harvard Business Review Press, Cambridge, MA

2 Richardson, Joan (2004) *From the Inside Out: Learning From Positive Deviance in Your Organization*, National Staff Development Council, Oxford, OH

3 Richardson, Joan (2004) *From the Inside Out: Learning from the Positive Deviance of your organization*, National Staff Development Council, Oxford, OH

4 Heath, Chip and Heath, Dan (2010) *Switch: Don't solve problems – copy success*, Crown Publishing, Brunswick, OH

5 Mathews, Ryan and Wacker, Watts (2004) *The Deviant's Advantage: How to use fringe ideas to create mass markets*, Crown Publishing, Brunswick, OH

Online resources

The Positive Deviance Initiative's website (www.positivedeviance.org) is an excellent online resource for all Positive Deviance topics. Among the many resources, it has a short summary of the approach that can be downloaded for free.

The Centre for Positive Organizational Scholarship can be found here: www.centreforpos.com

REFERENCES

Adams, M (1998) *Change Your Questions, Change Your Life*, John Wiley and Sons, New York

Buckingham, M (2005) What great managers do, *Harvard Business Review*, March, **83** (3), pp 70–79

Csíkszentmihályi, M (1990) *Flow: The psychology of optimal experience*, Harper and Row, New York

De Bono, E (2000) *Six Thinking Hats*, Penguin Books, London

Deming, W (1950) *Some Theory of Sampling*, John Wiley and Sons, New York

Deming, W (1982) *Quality, Productivity, and Competitive Position*, MIT, Cambridge, MA

Fredrickson, B (1998) What good are positive emotions? *Review of General Psychology*, **2**, pp 300–19

Goldratt, E and Cox, J (1986) *The Goal: A process of ongoing improvement*, North River Press, Great Barrington, MA

Immelt, J (2007) Six Sigma: So Yesterday? *Businessweek*, 10 June: www.businessweek.com/stories/2007-06-10/six-sigma-so-yesterday

Jackson, P and McKergow, M (2007) *The Solutions Focus: Making coaching and change SIMPLE*, (2nd rev edn), Nicholas Brealey Publishing, London

Kaplan, R and Norton, D (1996) *The Balanced Scorecard: Translating strategy into action*, Harvard Business Review Press

Kotter, J (1996) Leading change: why transformation efforts fail, *Harvard Business Review*, **73** (2), pp 59–67

Lewin, K (1946) Action research and minority problems, *Journal of Social Issues*, **2** (4), pp 34–46, DOI: 10.1111/j.1540-4560.1946.tb02295.x

Sinek, S (filmed September 2009, posted May 2010) How great leaders inspire action, *TED Talks* (accessed October 2012): http://www.ted.com/talks/simon_sinek_how_great_leaders_inspire_action.html

Six Sigma's Dummies Cheat Sheet: http://www.dummies.com/how-to/content/six-sigma-for-dummies-cheat-sheet.html

Stavros, J and Hinrichs, G (2009) *The Thin Book of SOAR: Building strengths-based strategy*, Thin Book Publishing, Bend, OR

Suzaki, K (1993) *The New Shop Floor Management: Empowering people for continuous improvement*, The Free Press, New York

Suzaki, K (2002) *Results from the Heart: How mini-company management captures everyone's talents and helps them find meaning and purpose at work*, The Free Press, New York

Taylor, F (1911) *The Principles of Scientific Management*, Harper and Brothers, New York and London

Tuckman, B (1965) Developmental sequence in small groups, *Psychological Bulletin*, **63** (6), pp 384–99

Whitney, D and Torsten-Bloom, A (2002) *The Power of Appreciative Inquiry: A practical guide to positive change*, Berrett-Koehler, San Francisco, CA

Womack, J and Jones, D (2003) *Lean Lexicon* (2nd edn), Lean Enterprise Institute, Cambridge, MA

Womack, J, Jones, D and Roos, D (1990) *The Machine That Changed the World: The story of lean production – Toyota's secret weapon in the global car wars that is now revolutionizing world industry*, HarperCollins, New York

Zandin, K and Maynard, H (2001) *Maynard's Industrial Engineering Handbook*, (5th rev edn), McGraw-Hill, New York and London

INDEX